The Artist's **Giclée*** Handbook

*Fine Art Digital Reproduction

Written by Susan Fader

Ditto Editions, LLC, Salem, Massachusetts
www.artistsgicleehandbook.com

September, 2010

Copyright © 2010 by Susan Fader

Published in the United States of America 2010
by Susan Fader, Ditto Editions, LLC
Salem, Massachusetts

Edited by Eileen Fritsch

Design & layout: Linda Coe

All photographs, including original art scans, by Nick Fader

ISBN 978-1-4507--3333-5

First Edition
Printed and bound in the USA by Velocity Print Solutions

About the Author

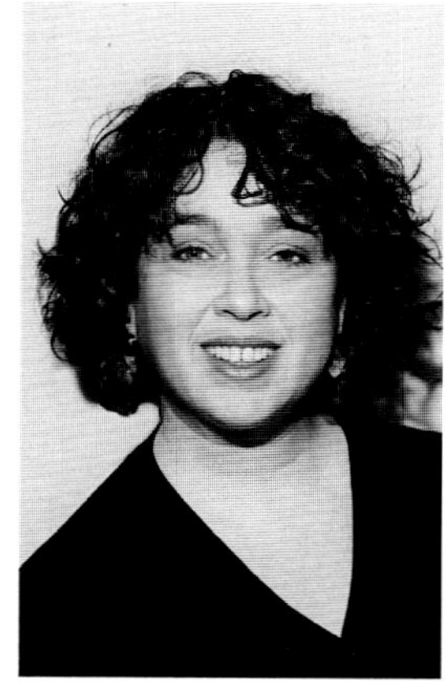

Susan Fader co-owns Ditto Editions, LLC in Salem Massachusetts with her husband Nick Fader. A graduate of Philadelphia College of Art with a Bachelor of Fine Art degree, Susan headed the advertising department of a large retail chain before opening her own agency in 1980, followed by 15 years spent working in consumer marketing and promotion. Susan has combined these experiences working with artists and in writing this book.

Devoted to the successful growth of the digital fine art reproduction world, Susan is focused on guiding artists in all aspects of creating, marketing and selling their prints. She believes that artists wishing to have success selling reproductions require a clear understanding of the process that creates them. It is her goal that this book, written specifically for artists, will serve as a guide.

Susan speaks regularly on the topic of Digital Fine Art Reproduction and Art Marketing. She has been a guest speaker at The Salmagundi Club in New York; the Scientific Illustrators Guild and the Bert Gallery, in Providence, Rhode Island; and to classes at Leslie College, Montserrat College of Art, and at Boston University's Center for Digital Imaging Arts as well as countless art associations around New England.

Table of Contents

Image Credits and Descriptions

All photos have been taken by Nick Fader and Caitlin Malone of Ditto Editions, LLC. All prints shown were digitized at 300 mega pixels and printed by Ditto Editions, LLC.

Chapter 1
Sunrise at Half Moon Beach
by Ray Crane,
www.raycranestudio.com
Oil on canvas, 12" x 20"
Printed on Fredrix 901WR canvas

Chapter 2
Lithographic version
by Giuseppe Elena (1775-1860)
of a painting by Pelagio Palagi.

Chapter 3
Digital Capture Studio including
large-format camera with digital
scanning back.

Chapter 4
Artist Gloria Najecki,
www.glorianajecki.com
Shown proofing her work;
center is *Fresh Air Trucker*,
acrylic on canvas 32" x 24"
Printed on Fredrix 901WR canvas

Chapter 5
Summer Feast
by Norman Laliberté,
www.laliberteprints.com
Shown printing on an Epson
Stylus® Pro using 60" Innova
Smooth Cotton White, 315gsm

Chapter 6
Shown: Detail of 26" x 11.5" Mono-print
by Claire Hurst
Printed on 36" Innova Textured
White, 315gsm

Chapter 7
Artist, Ginny Nickerson,
www.ginnynickerson.com
Shown with Susan Fader of Ditto Editions,
LLC, viewing packaged prints made from
the artist's original pastel paintings.

Chapter 8
Print on canvas of original 11" x 14"
oil on canvas, cello bagged and shown
with a romance card and unique
coordinating bag with label.

Dedication

This book is dedicated to my husband and business partner, Nick Fader, expert printmaker and artist. His talent, experience, and devotion to our company and the future of the digital fine art reproduction process was the motivation for my writing this book.

Acknowledgements

The first thank you goes to my Technical Editor, Eileen Fritsch, whose involvement and keen understanding of this subject perfectly matched my vision.

A big thank you goes to each of the following people whose involvement honored me and contributed to the sheer pleasure of this experience: Emily Schwartz, my Book Intern, whose patience and organization I could not have been without; Linda Coe, who adeptly took my design goals and translated them to so much more; Brian LeClair, Intellectual Property Attorney, who was kind enough to edit the section on copyright; Carol Rosengarten for proofreading the final manuscript, and protecting me from potential "Oh, no!" moments; and, to the Ditto Editions staff for their understanding during the long process of writing this book.

Preface

The concept that art should not be limited to the elite has been around since the Industrial Revolution. But the idea has gained fresh momentum now that digital technologies, inks, and print materials have made it economically feasible to print affordable reproductions that are not only incredibly accurate, but also long-lasting.

The demand for high-quality art reproductions is exploding for two reasons:

- If more people can afford to buy quality reproductions, then more artists (including yourself!) will be able to increase their earnings selling art.

- Creating high-quality copies of your original art can make more people familiar with your work. And the more people who see your work, the more likely you are to connect with people who may want to buy your originals.

Unfortunately, a lot of confusion and frustration currently exists in the market. As the demand for art-reproduction services has grown, so has the number of individuals offering the service. Some people with related backgrounds (such as commercial printers and photographers) add art reproduction as another revenue source. However, they generally underestimate the need for very specific technology and knowledge needed to do it well. They use the word "giclée" to promote their services without fully understanding that their background may not have fully prepared them to reproduce art as it can and should be done. Thus, they inadvertently add to the confusion.

These inexperienced providers of fine-art reproduction services simply do not realize that owning some of, or close to the right technology isn't enough to be able to produce the type of high-quality prints that you and your customers should be getting.

Compounding the problem is the fact that there are no official guidelines or commonly accepted standards for quality in fine art reproduction. Nor are there any regulatory bodies or associations watching out for the best interests of the artist or art reproduction print buyer.

As a result, many artists have had some unpleasant and stressful experiences digitally reproducing their art. They've wasted a lot of valuable time and money on unacceptable prints.

Some people jump to the mistaken conclusion that digital printing technology is inadequate, without understanding that fine art reproduction is a learned and mastered craft. Some printmaking studios have the experience and skills to do it well; others do not.

In this handbook, I'll explain everything you need to know to get the best possible art reproductions and market them in a way that will help you meet your goals as an artist.

You will see how far fine-art reproduction has evolved throughout history and learn about previous efforts to ensure that owning quality art was available to everyone. I will also discuss the widespread and unfortunate confusion over the term "giclée," recommend some alternatives, and explain why the use of the term should perhaps be reconsidered.

I will not bore you with too much technical detail. My goal is simply to give you enough knowledge of the process to help you make smart choices that result in prints you will be proud to sell. I want to help you reduce (or eliminate) the amount of time and money you waste, so you can spend more time doing what you love—creating more art.

A Few Things to Know
Before Reading This Handbook

The views, comments and explanations in this book are mine. They are
derived from my years as an artist, professional marketer, and digital fine art
reproduction printmaker. At this point in time, no official standards or
guidelines exist for the fine art reproduction business. Nor is there any
governing organization, such as an industry association. The lack of quality
standards is disheartening to those of us who have specialized in digital
printmaking for a number of years and have helped to perfect the process.
This book is not intended to be a substitute for these sorely needed standards
but is simply intended to give artists interested in fine-art digital reproductions
a starting point and reference source.

Writing this book was a labor of love. In my work at Ditto Editions, LLC
I have spoken with many artists who feel overwhelmed due to their lack of
understanding of the process. Some have inferior prints and do not even
realize it.

One of my goals with this book is to correct some of the biggest
misconceptions and to help people understand that digital reproductions
of fine art is an ideal way to provide *more art for more people while
providing more exposure and income for the artist.*

This book was written for a very specific audience—the artist who uses paints,
pastels, graphite, or other media to create one-of-a-kind 2D originals. This book
was not intended for digital photographers.

Starting with a digital image is far different than reproducing art originally created in other mediums. Making reproductions of a painting requires a unique process (and workflow), specific knowledge, skills, and experience. However, I hope artists who use different digital techniques and software to create original art on their computers will find this handbook helpful.

Doing this process well and responsibly is a learned and mastered art. In addition to technical skills, it requires a true love of art, and an appreciation of those who create it.

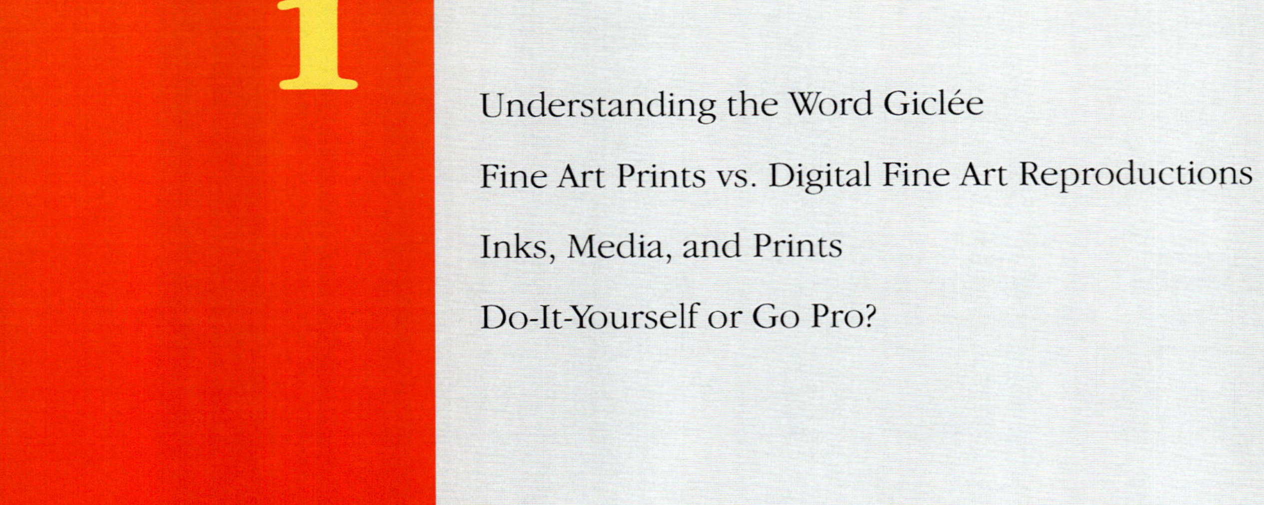

1

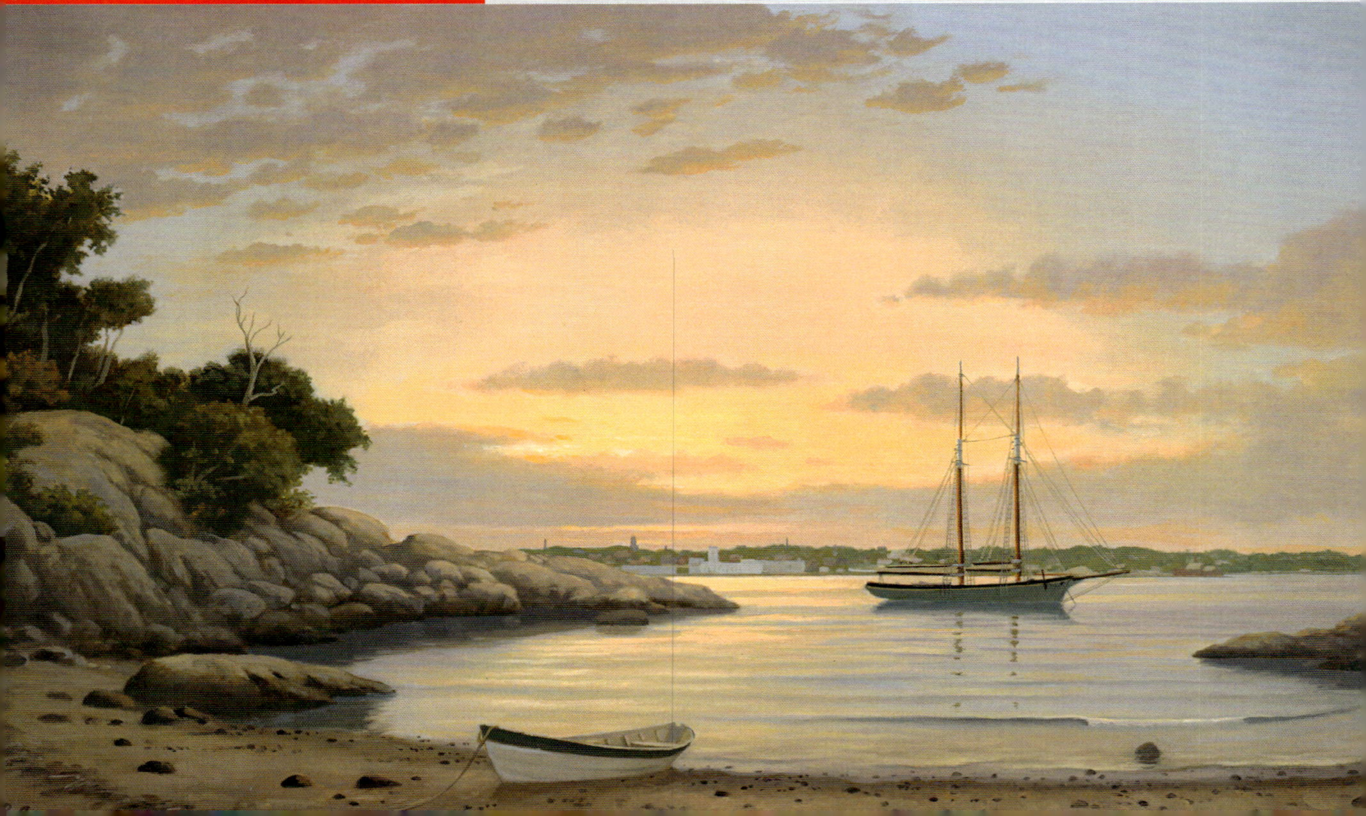

Moving Away from the Term "Giclée"

Digital printing systems today can reproduce art at quality levels far beyond what was possible just 10 or 15 years ago when the word "Giclée" was first adopted. "Giclée" has become the generic term used for anything that is a copy of artwork. It is generally assumed that the word describes a specific process and the resulting prints. No single definition can exist, because there are no official guidelines to ensure that "giclée" prints are made only from properly prepared files and printed using inks and materials that produce long-lasting prints.

Understanding the Word "Giclée"

The term "giclée" was originally coined in the early 1990s to describe reproductions of original paintings made on an expensive, revolutionary piece of inkjet-printing equipment (the Iris 3047). We'll talk more about the origins of the word "giclée" in the next chapter.

Meanwhile, the digital art-reproduction field has advanced so rapidly (and without any official standards or guidelines) that many artists I work with feel totally overwhelmed and confused or have had bad experiences trying to get "giclée" prints made of their work.

None of this surprises me because, in my opinion, the word "giclée" is both overused and grossly misunderstood. There is so much confusion surrounding the term "giclée" that I see it as a hindrance. The full acceptance of this form of reproduction by galleries and collectors is in question. Other names have been used as well as "giclée" such as pigmented prints. The acceptance of a more accurate name to describe today's process and the resulting prints is needed to help build confidence in digital fine art reproductions. As you will see, I have chosen to use "digital fine art reproduction" throughout this book.

Once the term "giclée" started becoming synonymous with high-end art, some photographers and photo labs started using the word to market photographic prints made on watercolor papers or canvas. At the same time, some artists started making color copies or prints on low-cost home printers and selling them as "giclées."

The generic use of the term to describe art prints has had some adverse effects. Many galleries have decided to play it safe by refusing to handle any digital fine art reproductions at all.

In addition, the art-buying public has no way of knowing whether the "giclée" prints sold in the racks of art-retail and art-association stores will last as long as they might expect or are of respectable reproduction quality. Some so-called "giclées" made on color copiers or with the wrong types of inks can fade quickly. Some ink colors in the print might fade more quickly than others causing all of the colors in the print to "shift" and look blue or pink.

The good news is there are signs of change among art retailers as more people start to understand the difference between a true quality digital reproduction and a poorly made print. While it can be less obvious to the untrained eye, it is best to be aware of some things that can indicate a poorly produced print. It is also difficult to see and evaluate the print fully without the original present, even for the artist.

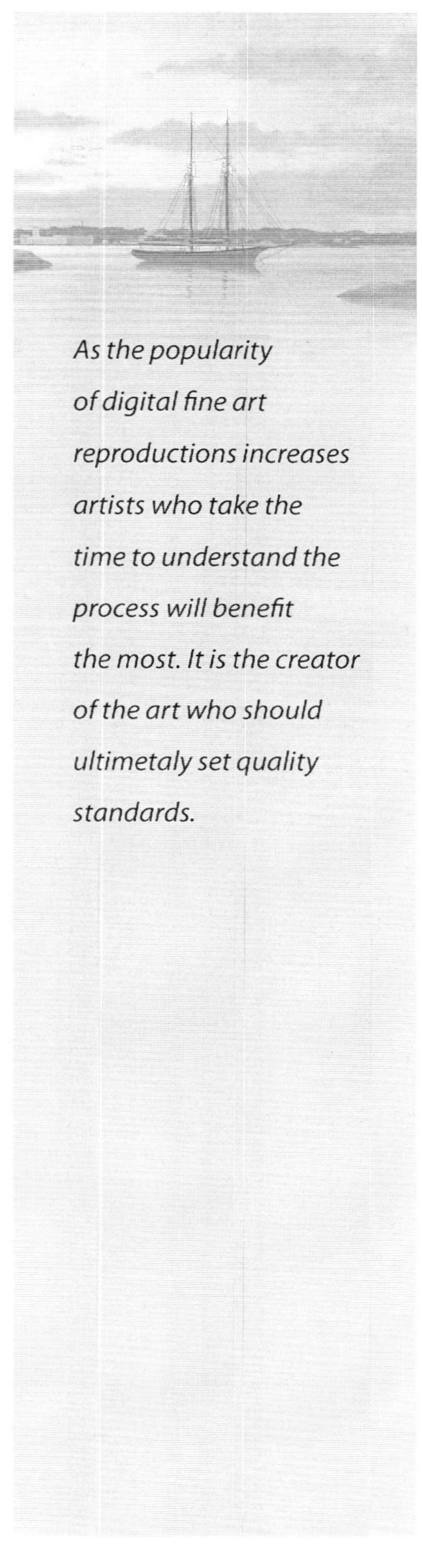

Fine Art Prints vs. Digital Fine Art Reproductions

Different types of printing techniques (e.g. monoprints, mezzotints, woodblocks, and etchings) are used by artists to create original art. There is a vast difference between the type of printmaking used to create fine art prints and the type of printing used for the express purpose of reproducing art.

While professionals in the art world know the difference, it is everyone's responsibility to use the terminology clearly and consistently. Referring to a reproduction as a fine-art print is not correct and not fair to artists who create hand crafted fine-art prints. Fine-art digital printmaking (without the word "reproduction") is also unfair to digital artists.

This is a good time to mention that another form of digital fine art printmaking exists. Some artists are using digital printers in combination with other art materials and techniques to make what might be considered digital monoprints. This is wonderful and exciting work; however, in this book, we are going to focus only on printing "reproductions" in which the prints we talk about are copies of original art. Original art can not only include two-dimensional art created in almost any medium but also original fine-art prints made through processes such as monoprinting or etching. It is not uncommon for an etcher or a monoprinter to have his or her favorite "pull" reproduced digitally. When you consider that the plates used in these other types of processes will eventually wear out, digital printing is a great way of extending the life of an original art print and storing a file that can be printed in the future.

Inks, Media, and Prints

Many artists proudly state their prints are archival. But what does that really mean?

The word "archival" comes from the root word archive which refers to a collection, such as a set of documents. Webster's defines "archival quality" as *"Materials that have been manufactured of inert materials specifically designed to extend the life of artifacts and records by protecting them from agents or deterioration."*

No period of time is associated with the word. However, using information they have been given by their printmaker or the companies that made their printer, inks, or papers, some artists will claim that their prints will last a certain period of time.

Print-permanence testing exists and print-life projections are being made, but this is a very complex subject and does not cover all of the different combinations of media and ink types that can be used to make prints.

Some artists may not realize that it is not enough to use archival media. For maximum longevity, archival pigment inks must also be used. Prints produced with an archival pigment ink on one type of media may last 80 years. When that same ink is used with a different type of media, the life of the print can approach 150 years.

It is important to understand that not every combination of inks and media have been tested. Making print-life claims is further complicated by the fact that the print must be displayed in a way that protects it from extreme exposure to excessive amounts of light, humidity, heat, and airborne pollutants. This is when working with an honest, reputable fine art digital printmaker is helpful. The most expert printmakers only offer papers and canvases that they purchased from knowledgeable, reliable sources they have used successfully for a number of years.

In Chapter 5, we will go into more details about inks and media and provide advice that can help you choose the right type of papers for specific types of artworks.

Do-It-Yourself or Go Pro?

Making and selling low-quality unstable copies of your art is not good business. If the prints you sell quickly fade or shift colors, your reputation as an artist will suffer. This can diminish your ability to sell better prints and even originals.

If you decide to print your own reproductions, you will also face limitations in the size and quality of the prints you can reproduce because you will not be using the higher-end capture equipment, specialized lighting systems, and printers that professional printmakers use to create and reproduce your files.

If you choose to print small copies of your art on paper, it is better to use a flatbed scanner than a digital SLR camera to convert your original art into a digital file. You are less likely to encounter lighting-related difficulties and other technical issues if you use a good-quality flatbed scanner.

To reduce the risk that your prints will fade prematurely, use a pro-model desktop or wide-format printer that uses pigment inks with digital fine-art paper from a trusted manufacturer.

Whether you are making prints yourself or hiring a professional, it is important to understand this basic principle: A bad file cannot produce a good print.

If you do not have a basic familiarity with the requirements of digital prepress and color management, it will be very hard for you to generate the top-quality file that is needed to print high-quality reproductions that will best represent the beauty and visual impact of your originals.

<table>
<tr><td colspan="3">FIG. 1.1 — CREATING A DIGITAL FINE ART REPRODUCTION</td></tr>
<tr><th>PRODUCTION STEP</th><th>PURPOSE</th><th>CHAPTER</th></tr>
<tr><td>Capture digital "scan"</td><td>Preparing the file from which the final prints will be run.</td><td>Chapter 3</td></tr>
<tr><td>Proofing</td><td>Examining proofs for issues that may affect the final print such as focus and color. Making adjustments and re-checking.</td><td>Chapter 4</td></tr>
<tr><td>Before Printing</td><td>Selecting media print and edition sizes.</td><td>Chapter 5</td></tr>
<tr><td>Printing</td><td>The final approved file is readied and prints are run.</td><td>Chapter 5</td></tr>
<tr><td>Finishing</td><td>Prints are trimmed and packed; and the additional steps of coating and stretching canvas prints are performed.</td><td>Chapter 5</td></tr>
</table>

2

Evolution of Early Techniques

Digital Printing

Digital Fine Art Reproduction Printing

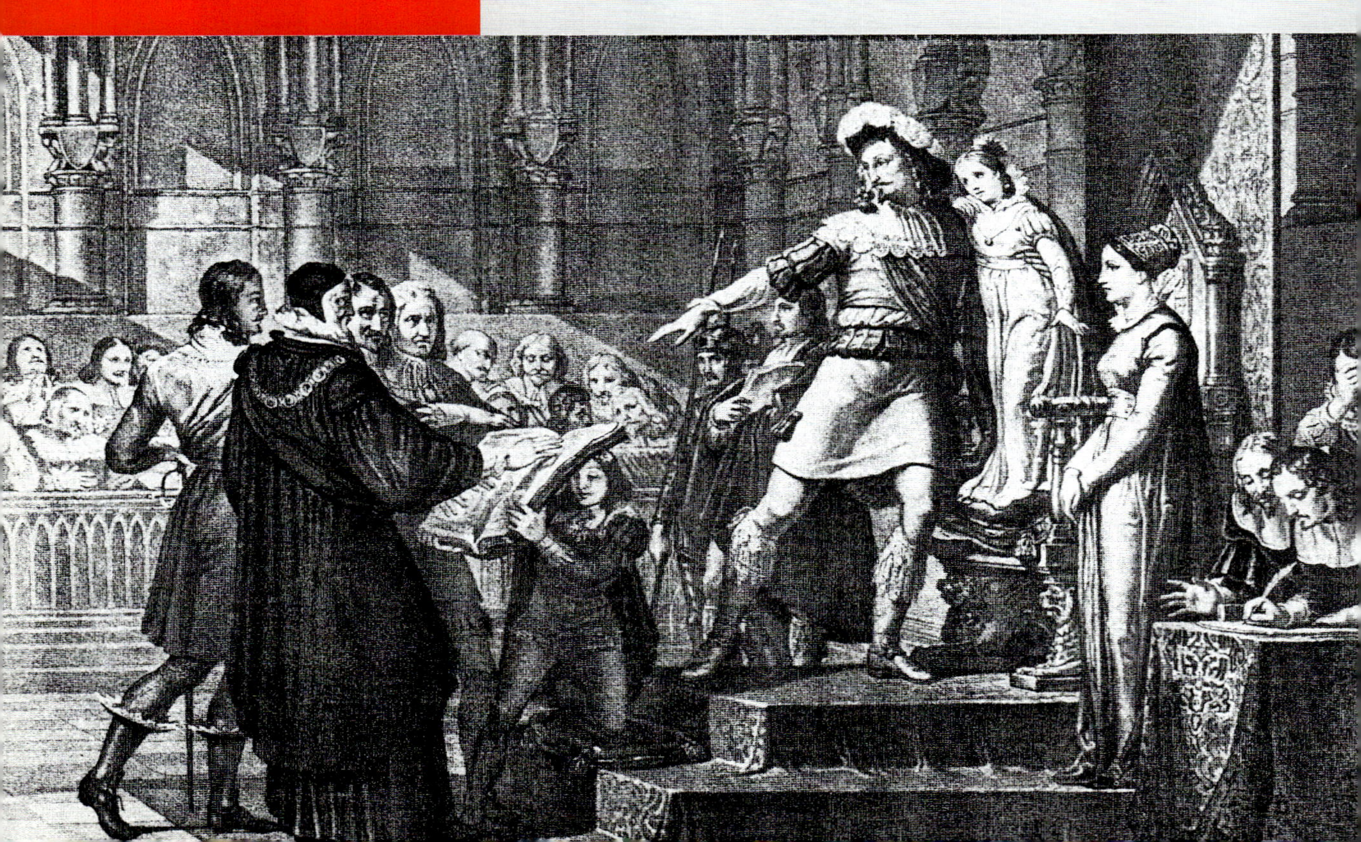

A Short History of Art Reproduction

In order to better appreciate today's amazing digital-reproduction technologies, let us take a quick look at how paintings have been reproduced in the past. As you will see, artists have always recognized the value of creating copies of their work. And you will see that the techniques for making reproductions have constantly evolved and improved. But until now, most options for reproducing art with accuracy and precision have had some limitations.

Evolution of Early Techniques

Engravings:

The first prints created with the specific intention of making multiple copies of an image were made from engravings and etchings. These "depictions" of paintings enabled artists to make and sell multiple copies of a single image.

The Intaglio engraving method of making prints was invented in Germany by the 1430s, and involved using a press to transfer ink from the recessed grooves of an engraved printing plate to paper. One artist who benefitted from this process was the German artist Israhel van Meckenam (1445 -1503) who was known for his ability to distribute and sell prints of his artwork. Selling depictions of paintings helped create a greater awareness and appreciation of art among the general public. Public interest in art blossomed in the fifteenth century and the demand for depictions of original paintings grew.

Some of the famous artists who created depictions of their paintings were Titian (1488-1576) and Raphael (1483-1520) who began collaborating with printmakers to make prints of their art. The artistic and commercial success of these partnerships made copying paintings for the sole purpose of reproductive prints a growing business. Even though quality varied greatly, the success of reproduction prints came to dominate the market in Italy in the sixteenth century.

During the seventeenth century, printmaking for the purpose of art reproduction continued to increase. Rubens (1577-1640), like Titian, depended on trained engravers working exclusively for him as a way to control the final print quality.

Techniques for reproductive printmaking continued to develop in the eighteenth century. In England, artist William Hogarth (1697-1764) is known to have been exceedingly successful at selling reproductions of his paintings. His reproductions were priced to reach a middle- to upper-working-class market.

Aquatint:

By the nineteenth century, the ability to create a "tone" in an etching was invented by French artist, Jean Baptiste Le Prince (1734–1781). The technique known as aquatint provided printmakers with a way to add more nuances to their etchings. Over the course of the nineteenth century reproduction prints of watercolors began to look more closely like the originals. One of the first artists to take full advantage of the potential of aquatint was Goya (1746-1828). He was also an early adopter of the next evolution in printing—lithography.

Lithography and Chromolithography:

Lithography was invented in 1796 and quickly evolved into chromo-lithography, a method of making multi-color prints. Lithography is a printing method in which the image is transferred from a smooth stone or metal plate. Chromolithography involved using multiple plates—one plate per color. Chromolithography replaced the need to hand-color prints and became a popular method of printing posters and greeting cards in the nineteenth century. It was also viewed as the best method for replicating an original painting. Doing it well, however, was a real craft, because each color in a "chomo" required making a separate stone (plate). After the image was drawn on the stone, the stone was treated with certain chemicals and the plate was inked with oil-based paints and passed through a printing press. If a painting used 25 colors, the paper used to make each reproduction would need to be passed through the printing press 25 times. For each pass, the new plate on the press had to be in perfect alignment ("registration") with the colors previously printed with the other plates. Because the process was so time-consuming and demanding, it's not surprising that not all art reproductions were of equal quality. And like today, the production of some inferior art reproductions led some people to question the viability of the reproduction process itself.

In the 1850s the use of photography for making lithographic plates led to the invention of offset lithography, which by the late nineteenth century became the standard method used for all commercial and fine art reproduction. "Offset" lithography is the process in which the image on the smooth plate is transferred to a flexible sheet for transfer to the printing paper. Until the end of the twentieth century offset lithography was the primary process used for fine art reproduction. And it is still the most practical and economical way to produce tens of thousands of copies of a single image.

Serigraphy:
Another type of printing that has been used to reproduce art is serigraphy, a painterly printing method that evolved from the screen-printing processes originally developed for industrial purposes. In screen printing, a roller or squeegee is moved across an ink-blocking stencil attached to a woven mesh. The motion of the squeegee forces ink through the open areas of the mesh onto the print surface. Serigraphy enables ink to be applied in different thicknesses and opacities.

Before the 1900s, artists began to use screen printing both to create original works and as a repeatable medium for duplicating images. Interest in serigraphy grew in the twentieth century after the development of photographic screens made it possible to reproduce images with a high level of detail. The main drawback to using serigraphy as a method of reproducing paintings is that it can be very labor-intensive, because a new screen must be created for every color, so like chromolithography, serigraphy requires each color to be laid down in perfect registration. Because it is derived from industrial printing on multiple substrates, serigraphy involves the use of harsh chemicals and emulsions. Serigraphers who disliked using these chemicals were among the first to experiment with environmentally friendly, aqueous-ink digital printing technologies that could reproduce art on a wide range of papers and textiles.

Digital Printing

In the 1990s, artists and photographers began experimenting with inkjet printing which doesn't require the time or expense of setting up different plates for different colors. In inkjet printing, sophisticated software controls the sequence and patterns of how tiny droplets of inks are laid down and mixed to form colors. The final result is a continuous-tone print.

With lithography or serigraphy, the time and expense of creating the plates and screens made it very expensive for artists to order just one or two prints at a time. The only artists who could afford to make reproductions were those who were confident they could sell (and/or store) hundreds of copies of each piece. Plus, every print had to be the exact same size.

Inkjet printing (digital fine art reproduction) made it possible for artists to reproduce their work a few prints at a time without having to invest thousands of dollars to make large print runs of a single piece of artwork and owning the entire edition in advance of selling. Another significant advantage is that the print sizes can be varied to provide the artist with more selling options per image.

Although artists were quick to recognize the potential benefits of inkjet printing for art reproduction, the first large-format inkjet printers were not designed to produce images that would last. After learning more about the type of print performance that artists and photographers would require, printer manufacturers started researching and developing the inks and printing technologies that would be more suitable for reproducing art. Modern printers deliver wider color gamuts, higher resolutions, and ink-and-media combinations that can last for well over 100 years. These more advanced inkjet-printing systems started hitting the market around the year 2000.

Electrographic digital-printing systems (laser-printers, color-copiers, digital presses) use different types of toners and electrostatically charged plates to print images. Although efforts are currently underway to make longer-lasting toners, copiers and commercial digital presses are not designed to accurately depict all of the nuances in the color range of a painting. They are designed mostly for on-demand printing of documents and marketing collateral that do not need to last for decades.

Hybrid digital printing systems that convert digital files into chromogenic photographic prints (Lambda, LightJet) are not the best choice for producing reproductions of paintings because they can only print on photo papers—not the canvases or watercolor and other fine art paper surfaces that match the type of material used to create the original work.

So let's get back to inkjet printing and talk more specifically about digital fine art "giclée" printing.

Digital Fine Art Reproduction Printing

"Giclée" printing is actually a highly specialized form of inkjet art reproduction and uses only those ink and media combinations that are projected to last for generations. But as we discussed in Chapter 1, the term has lost its original meaning because so many artists, photographers, galleries, and art organizations are using it inappropriately.

The term "giclée" was first coined in the early 1990s, when photographers first began to experiment with digitally outputting scanned images on the Iris 3047 continuous-tone inkjet printer. The Iris 3047 was a four-color printer that Iris Graphics developed for printing, reviewing, and approving hard-copy proofs of magazine, catalog, and advertising pages that were created digitally on desktop-publishing systems and saved on a floppy disk.

The first use of the Iris 3047 printer for artistic purposes began when photographers wanted a way to make large prints of scanned images edited in Photoshop. However, because Iris Graphics, Inc. originally designed the printer to produce disposable proofs, the four ink colors were not permanent. Even prints displayed behind glass started to fade or shift colors in fewer than five years.

Just as a group of artists chose the word "serigraphy" to distinguish artistic uses of screen-printing from industrial uses, fine-art printmakers adopted the term "giclée" to separate art reproductions made on the Iris 3047 from the commercial proofs the printer was intended to deliver. Derived from the French word "gicler" (meaning "to spurt or spray"), "giclée" was selected for its reference to the manner in which the inks spray onto the substrate running through the printer.

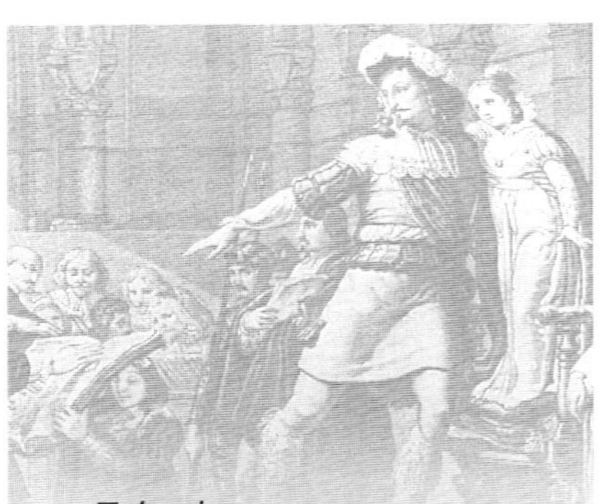

Take the same care when you create your digital fine art reproductions as you use in creating the original piece and sell them both with pride.

When correctly produced, the quality that is possible with "giclée printing" today goes far beyond what was possible in the 1990s. Not only are the printers far superior in terms of resolution, color gamut, and size, but the full digital-art reproduction process now entails a number of steps made possible through advancements in digital imaging, inks and substrates. With specific combination of inks and materials, quality inkjet prints can last well over 100 years and reproduce the tiniest nuances of detail.

For reasons described in Chapter 1, I think the time has come to move away from the term "giclée". Whereas the term was originally coined to describe art reproductions crafted with expertise on a specialized piece of inkjet-printing equipment the need for the proper equipment is still true today. It is unfortunate that some consumer-printer manufacturers now imply that hobbyists can use digital cameras and desktop inkjet printers to create their own "giclée prints."

When artists show and sell their digital fine art reproductions, they must find ways to let customers know that these reproductions were made from the finest combinations of imaging and printing techniques with materials that will last for generations to come.

3

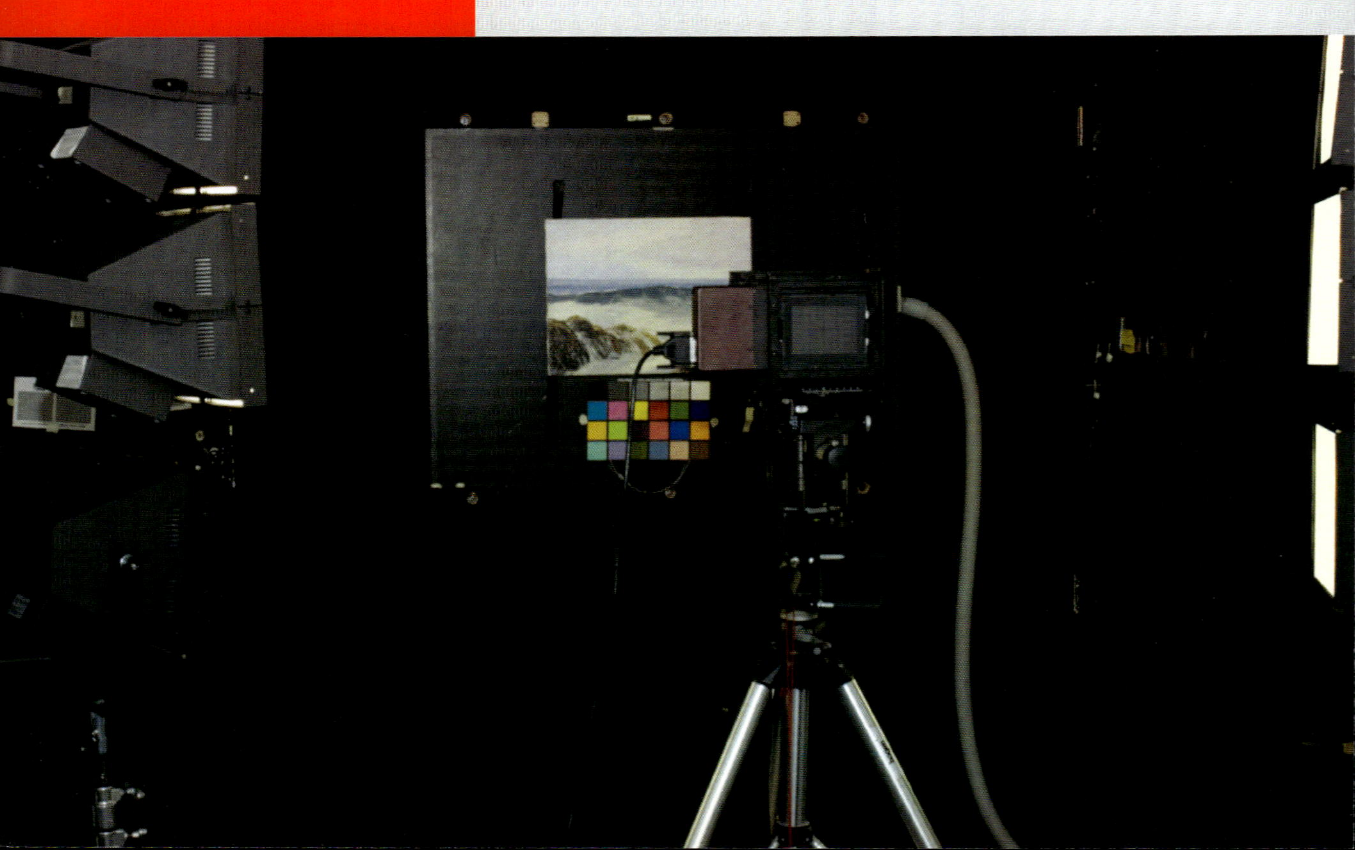

Creating the File for Printing

Consider this: Even if two different printmaking studios use exactly the same type of printer, the quality of your prints can easily be noticeably different.

Why? Because the key to achieving an incredibly accurate, high-quality reproduction does not reside solely with the type or model of the inkjet printer used. Rather, it depends primarily on the quality of the file that is sent to that printer. And the ability to create a quality art-reproduction file depends largely on the skill and experience of the printmaker, the ability to evaluate color and detail, and the digital pre-print processes used.

The Importance of the Digital File

In digital fine art reproduction, creating the digital file is where the craftsmanship comes in. Ultimately, how your final print looks will depend largely on how expertly your original art was converted into a digital file.

Garbage in, garbage out does not sound very nice, but it correctly conveys the fact that if you start with a file filled with hot spots, lack of sharpness, and inaccurate colors, then your print will contain these faults, too. Over working the file in photoshop to correct these problems only compromises the file quality further.

In this chapter, we will look at the different types of equipment that can be used to convert your original art into a digital file. Then, we will talk more about some of the specialized steps required to get the best possible results from the digital equipment. We will briefly discuss some of the steps required to prepare the digital file for proofing.

At the end of this chapter, I hope you will have a better understanding of why your final results will only be as good as the individual who performs the work. Creating an excellent file for art reproduction requires in-depth expertise in the controls, lighting, and software used in conjunction with the equipment used to "capture" a digital image of your original art.

Types of Capture Equipment

Many different types of scanners and cameras can be used to make digital files for printing. However, all of these capture devices are not appropriate for making accurate copies of an original painting or other 2D artwork. There is a huge difference between making a digital file for everyday printing of documents and photographs vs. creating a digital file that will reproduce all of the gorgeous textures, brush strokes, and color nuances in fine art.

That does not mean that only the most expensive equipment must be used to reproduce art. It is important however, to understand the differences between the major types of capture devices and to know which ones can produce the level of quality you and your customers expect for the type of art you produce. Then, you need to know more about the experience and expertise of the individual who will be capturing the work.

Keep in mind that your goal should be to have a digital file that is as perfect as possible at the time of capture. The less editing that is required, the better your final print will be. In addition, you can use that file to produce prints in a variety of sizes, as website images, and for promotional materials such as brochures and show announcements.

Types of Scanners

The three main types of scanners are drum, flatbed, and reprographic (table or wide-format) scanners.

Drum scanners:
These devices, invented in 1957, were first used in commercial prepress and photo labs because they could scan both prints and slides. Originals up to 11 x 17-in. are mounted on an acrylic "drum" which rotates at high speeds in front of optics that deliver image information.

Because drum scanners are used mostly with film, drum scanners are not a good choice for art reproduction. Using a film camera to create slides or transparencies of original art isn't recommended because film has its own color space and grain. This makes it less likely that the print will be true to the original art. So, be wary of a printmaking studio that claims to be able to make "museum-quality" fine-art reproductions from your transparencies or slides.

Commercial and desktop flatbed scanners:

In a flatbed scanner, the original art is placed on a glass pane that is illuminated from below. An opaque cover shuts out the ambient light while the image is captured by a moving set of sensors with red, green, and blue filters.

While "pro-model" flatbed scanners have become increasingly affordable, they still offer a limited ability to control resolution, light, and focus. Thus, flatbed scanners are best suited for making copies of small, flat art without texture that will be printed at the same size or close to it. Most flatbed scanners are not appropriate for large works of art because you still have to make multiple scans of any art that is bigger than the scanning bed. These files would then have to be matched up and joined digitally ("stitched") to create the file for printing.

To minimize the likelihood that any digital "noise" will show up in your print, it's best to use a capture system that can capture your original at actual size.

Cruse Synchron Table Scanners:

Cruse is a German company that has been making specialized large-format image capture devices since 1979. The equipment was originally designed for institutions and organizations that needed a non-contact method of replicating large-format prints such as maps, drawings, and rare, fragile documents.

In Cruse devices, the original is placed on a mechanized table that passes beneath a scan head that provides stable illumination for digitizing flat art and large documents. Very few printmaking studios can afford these expensive, industrial-grade reprographic scanners, particularly the larger units that can scan large items. Fortunately, equivalent results of large originals can usually be achieved with a large-format scanning-back camera in the hands of a true expert.

Types of Digital Cameras

We are not even going to talk about using film cameras to make art reproductions because creating a slide or transparency that must be scanned before making the print file adds extra unnecessary steps to the process that degrades the quality of the file.

The advantage to using the digital-camera process to capture an image of your original art is that you aren't restricted by the size of the flatbed on your scanner. You can position the original on a "copy stand" and take the shot. That sounds easy in theory, but, unfortunately it is not that simple. The file quality will be greatly affected by two key elements: the resolution the digital camera is capable of creating and the type and quality of the lighting used.

Starting with a low resolution file makes it more difficult, if not impossible, to make high-quality, large-format prints. The use of special software to create extra pixels of information for color management or to hold super-fine details is necessary, but this type of software is not desirable because the software will degrade the file quality. We will go into more detail about lighting later, but how the original is lit when it is digitized affects how the colors look and how well textures and details will be reproduced in the final print.

Currently, three major types of equipment are being used to photograph art:

DSLRs:
Digital SLRs (single-lens reflex) cameras are widely used by professional photographers, artists, designers, and hobbyists. Made by various companies, they use different sizes of CCD or CMOS sensors to record image files of 8 to 22 megapixels.

Medium-Format Camera with a Digital Chip or Scanning Back:
These devices can record image files from 16 to 39 megapixels.

Large-Format Scanning Back:
These devices can create a 300-megapixel file in a single capture.

Hire an Art Reproduction Specialist

Even if you own a pro-model DSLR that can capture a 10-megapixel file, if you want to create a file that can be used for quality reproductions in large sizes, it is best not to even attempt to shoot your artwork yourself.

Hiring a professional photographer to capture your originals can also be risky because photographing an original work of art for reproduction is not the same as photographing a person, landscape or product. While most professional photographers understand the different techniques involved in shooting portraits and landscapes, many photography pros do not always understand the specialized techniques involved in lighting and photographing art for reproduction. Some professional photographers may have medium-format cameras, but they may not have the specialized lighting or knowledge to use it to achieve the best possible results in art reproduction. Do not confuse photography art for portfolios with imaging it for reproduction. The best option is to find a printmaking studio that has the large-format equipment and experience to handle all steps of the fine art reproduction process from start to finish.

The Advantage of a Closed-Loop Calibrated System

If you go to one source to have your images captured and then to another source to have your files printed, you're taking a chance that the final print will not be as good as today's technology allows. Work performed under one roof in a calibrated, "closed-loop" system is the best way to ensure that your colors are reproduced correctly and consistently at every stage of the process. That is because all of the equipment used in each stage of production will be functioning in the same "color space." It will also be easier to identify the source of any quality issues that may arise. Since each piece of equipment has been calibrated to the next, the file (and any adjustments to it) will remain consistent and unchanged throughout. For example, imagine taking a successful pastry recipe you have made at home many times and then baking it in a neighbor's oven. Because your ovens are not calibrated the same, the pastry baked at your neighbor's house may not look and taste the same.

If you go to two different sources for the capture and printing phases, each service provider will have different versions of editing software, different methods and standards of proofing, and different levels of knowledge of color and quality.

On the other hand, just because a printmaker has all the equipment needed to perform all phases of production under one roof, it does not necessarily make him qualified to handle your art reproduction work. You must make sure that the printmaker you hire is calibrating all of his equipment. For example when monitors are not properly calibrated to the rest of the equipment used in the capture-to-print workflow, the printmaker may be introducing new errors into the file during editing because the colors being viewed on the uncalibrated monitor are not really the colors that exist in the actual digital file.

Lighting the Original Artwork

In a flatbed scanner, the light is imparted by a scanning unit as it moves over the image. So one has no control over how the art is lit during capture.

When artwork is photographed with a camera, the lighting can be varied. It is usually determined by whatever type of equipment the photographer uses in his studio. A professional photographer using a DSLR to shoot images might use different types of strobe lights. If the artist tries to shoot the images himself, he would most likely use the light available in the room or sunlight from a nearby window.

To properly capture detail and texture, an experienced printmaker will typically use two movable light sources. Lights that can accommodate filters provide the most versatility and enable different techniques to be used with different varieties of art surfaces. This is particularly important when dealing with varnished art or with work that has irregular surface finishes. Not all lighting equipment is best or can be used with all types of digital capture methods. This may mean extra steps or conditions that can affect the outcome of the final prints or even the safety of the original. Protecting the original from damage is extremely important during the lighting stage. UV rays in light can damage art which is why museum visitors are asked not to use flashes when taking photographs.

Here are a few other things to look for when evaluating the quality of the printmaker's lighting system.

Even Lighting:
Is the light source casting light evenly over the entire image from edge to edge and corner to corner? Poorly balanced lighting is most often identified by inspecting the corners of the captured image or comparing one area to another. You should not be able to see a darker cast anywhere.

Highlights:

Are there hot spots in the image? Or tiny specks of lights known as spectral highlights? Hot spots can easily be noticed in the capture stage; they should be corrected before creating the final print. Spectral highlights are another matter. They can go unnoticed in the proofing stage by artists who are more focused on color or who are exuberant about seeing their work reproduced.

Highlights must be corrected when the file is displayed on the computer. Most printmakers can correct an obvious glare reasonably well or re-shoot the piece. But eliminating spectral highlights with post-capture software means that many pixels in the file are disturbed and altered. This is not a professional practice, and the integrity of the final print will be compromised. In this case, the digital capture must be redone.

The best solution is to prevent such problems by finding a professional printmaker who possesses the skills and lighting equipment to make sure that hot spots and spectral highlights never appear in the first place. For experienced printmakers these defects are a non-issue because they have invested in the time and equipment to prevent them. But when lighting-related issues are a concern, there is sure to be added work, so be prepared to discuss responsibility and added costs.

Color and Light:

Are the printmaker's lights as close to natural daylight as possible and appropriate for use in a controlled setting? This is important because the first steps toward achieving accurate color begins with proper lighting. An experienced professional knows that it is a necessary step to create a color profile prior to the final digitizing. When this step is taken for each piece of artwork, it can save a lot of time, money, and frustration that many associate with color proofing.

Restored art often includes wax and should never be exposed to hot lights that can soften the surface. Encaustic art can be badly damaged by incorrect lighting. I have seen the wax surface dripping off encaustic art that was exposed to excessively hot lights.

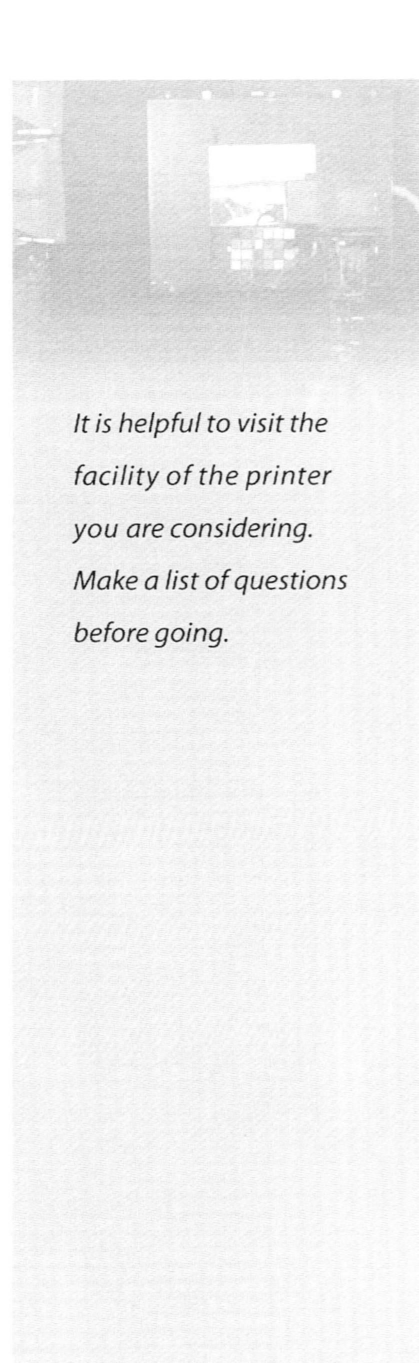

Preparing the File for Proofing

During this stage the printmaker takes care of special requests such as signature removal, image cropping, or digital repairs. Expect to pay an additional charge for these services, because they do involve some time.

In preparing the file for proofing, the best practice is to create proofs that are the same size as the original art. This provides the most accurate way to check for highlights of all types, focus, and color accuracy.

When an image is to be printed larger or smaller than the original, a second set of proofs at the altered size can be provided. This is typically done once the proofing work at actual size has been completed. To save money, avoid full proof prints, and request proofing strips as described in the following chapter.

4

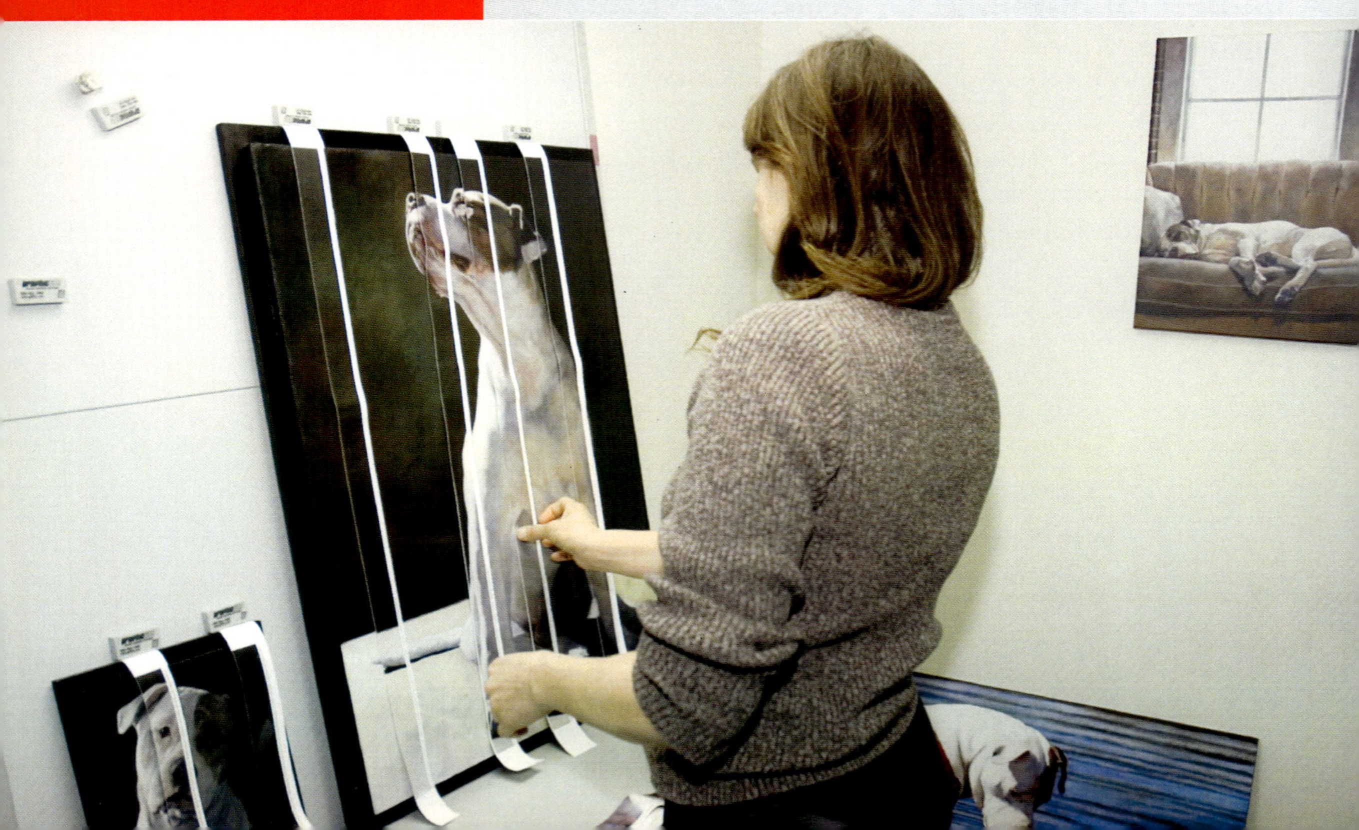

Understanding the Proofing Process

When performed correctly, proofing is the step that provides reassurances to the printmaker and the artist. It is a way for the printmaker to know he is meeting the client's goals. For you, the artist, proofing is the opportunity to be sure you will be satisfied with the final prints. The key to successful results is good communication between both parties.

I often hear from artists that proofing is less-than-an-enjoyable experience. While there are many specific factors that individuals may not have liked about their particular experiences, problems often boil down to a simple misunderstanding of the role each party should play in the process. In addition, expectations need to be clear and well managed. All of this can save time, money, and frustration.

Types of Proofs

Proofing is something many artists are unfamiliar with before their first experience with a printmaker. Many approaches to presenting and pricing proofs exist and every printmaker has his own way of doing it. So, it is smart to know the policies and pricing before a project begins. Below are some of the most common ways proofs are presented in digital fine-art reproduction.

Full Size Proofs:
If the printmaker offers (or the artist requests) a full-size proof, it is probably going to come at a significant cost. If there is a sensible reason to view the entire image, then do so. However, with other proofing techniques (and with proper guidance), proofing at full size should not be necessary.

Mini Proofs:
Another common approach is to print a reduced version of the original. Before agreeing to a "mini" proof, there are some issues to be considered. Most obvious is the fact that comparing a mini proof against the original is limiting. For example, consider the scale of the brush strokes at a reduced size. The change can make it more difficult to visually compare and judge color. In addition, smaller proofs can make it easier to miss defects such as highlights and out-of-focus areas that will be visible when the file is printed actual size.

Proofing Strips:
This is the method that avoids costly, wasteful use of materials but still offers 1:1 ratio comparisons. Proofing strips are typically three to four inches wide and the full length or width of the original. The size of the original determines the width of the strips and how many are needed for accurate viewing and decision making. Proofing strips should always be provided at actual size. Once approved, proofing strips can be created at the intended print size for review if necessary. This is a particularly good practice if the print size is significantly different than the size of the original art. The goal is to provide enough strips to allow you to check all areas, particularly the nuances of each color and texture.

In addition to being more cost-effective and time efficient, this method of proofing allows everyone involved the opportunity to review details more reliably.

One quick caveat: Stay away from "proofing paper"! Less experienced printmakers will sometimes try to show you proofs on a less costly substrate known as proofing paper. When this is done, proofs will not offer a reliable view of how the color will really look in the final prints. For accurate proofing and best results, never review proofs that are printed on anything other than the very same paper or canvas on which the final prints will be produced. Paper and canvas options are discussed in more detail in Chapter 5.

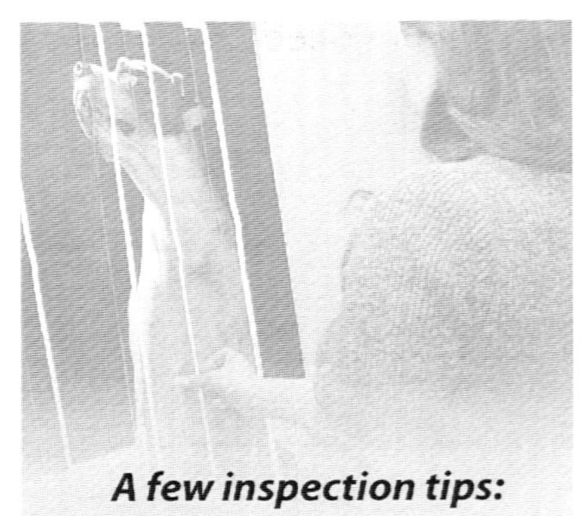

The Language of Color

Both the printmaker and the artist should be aware that they may be speaking different "languages" when it comes to describing color. When artists "proof", they are most comfortable describing color as they would paint.

The digital printmaker, on the other hand, is typically more inclined to speak about the color in technical terms. The language best used during proofing includes descriptive values such as cool or warm, light or dark. Avoid subjective or ambiguous terms that are open to individual interpretation.

Other more subtle problems may appear when talking about color, such as color casts, contrasts or saturation issues. In digital fine art reproduction, there are many different ways to make color adjustments, and a skilled printmaker will know which adjustment is most appropriate for the type of correction needed. A good printmaker should be an expert in all the areas listed in fig 4.1: The Language of Color.

During the capture phase of the art-reproduction process, a skilled printmaker will capture a color chart at the same time as each individual piece of art. When the print is proofed, this color chart information will provide the printmaker with valuable information regarding the nature of the colors in the capture. For instance, the printmaker can see if the whites are as neutral as they should be or if they contain a cast. This makes it possible to make color adjustments early in the process and eliminates "chasing-the-color," a common term used for the excessive and often frustrating time spent trying to match color. Most important, this step will prevent the file from becoming over manipulated which affects pixel quality and the quality of the final print.

FIG. 4.1 — THE LANGUAGE OF COLOR CHART

TECHNIQUES	USES
Masks	Used to isolate colors and ready them for adjustment without affecting other areas.
Curves	Used to adjust contrast and can also be used to add or subtract color*.
Hue and Saturation Tools	Used to raise or lower color intensity and also used to change the cast in a color*.
Selective Color	Allows the isolation of a specific color and then adjusts it using many of the tools already listed.

*Can be used with or without a mask

What to Expect

In an ideal world, the printmaker and artist would come to the proofing session with similar expectations of their individual roles. This doesn't always happen of course, but here is an ideal scenario:

The Printmaker's Role in the Proofing Process:
The printmaker would begin the session with proofs that are already created and ready to discuss. Then, without getting overly technical, the printmaker would educate the artist about certain discoveries and decisions that were made before the proofing session even began. The printmaker would guide the artist through every step of the proofing process, and respond to concerns and questions in a responsible and factual manner. The printmaker should agree to make any adjustments that are within the scope of reason and should have policies in place for dealing with any that are not attainable. A qualified printmaker should respond professionally when differences in opinion occur or when the project is not proceeding quite the way the printmaker and/or client had envisioned. For example, some colors may be "out of gamut" because the artist has used a pure or synthetic pigment that cannot be perfectly matched with inks. It helps for the printmaker to be open and clear about this fact.

The Artist's Role in the Proofing Process.
Ideally, the artist should come to the proofing session with a basic understanding of what to expect and realize that digital fine art reproduction is a process unlike any other form of printing. Before hiring the printmaker, the artist should have learned the fundamentals of the digital fine-art reproduction process.

Before reacting to any single concern with the proof, the artist should first look at the overall appearance of the print as compared to the original artwork. The artist should proof with patience, and carefully discuss the specifics of each concern, and engage with the printmaker to establish a clear understanding of what happens next. For a successful proofing session the artist should be aware that a fine line exists between color that is "off" or "not acceptable" and a color that should be considered satisfactory. The artist should understand that digital fine-art reproduction is a process that uses technology that may be new to them and that a learning curve can exist.

What Not To Accept

A red flag should go up if at a proofing session the artist sits at the computer with the printmaker while they work together to color correct a file.

A qualified printmaker should have already done the bulk of the color-correction in advance of the proofing session. When you hire a printmaker to perform professional services, you should not be expected to spend valuable time tweaking color and checking too many additional proofs. This is an indication that the printmaker was not prepared for your session.

Another red flag is when you are told that certain colors can not be perfect, or if the printmaker suggests that you purposely try not to match the original. Yes, it is true that some paint colors and types can not be matched including fluorescent, iridescent, pearlized, metallic and some "pure pigment" colors. But these issues should be fully discussed before the project begins. A qualified printmaker will be able to provide clear explanations of possible options and then produce a print that will be acceptable to you. If that does not seem possible, or if the communications are not going well, it may be wise to rethink whether moving forward is a good idea. A lot of frustration, extra time, and expense can be avoided if you have a good working relationship with your printmaker.

Keep in mind that it may be time to rethink the whole experience if you are asked to spend hours at a monitor tweaking colors instead of simply reviewing a printed proof and making a few adjustments. It is certainly time to look for a better printmaker if you feel you must accept anything less than 90-100% color match. Many artists have shown me prints that they were not completely satisfied with, and yet, they still paid their bill. I find this behavior puzzling. If you went to the dentist to cap a front tooth and it was not a good match to your other teeth, would you still pay the bill? In some cases, you may simply be dealing with someone who does not have the right combination of equipment or has insufficient experience or knowledge. We are not looking to point fingers or assign blame. These situations are due to the lack of professional standards and guidelines for digital fine-art reproduction.

The BAT

Every edition should start with a Bon a-Tier (BAT), or proof, that has been approved and signed by the artist. Bon a-Tier is a French term that means "good to print". Commonly used by fine art digital reproduction printmakers, its origins are much older and come from the etching process. In the etching process, the final and most perfect proof was reserved by the etcher as the model for making subsequent prints from the same plate. It would be the equivalent of the word "file" today.

In addition to the artist's signature as confirmation of approval, the BAT may include other information such as the date the proof was approved or details about how the file was printed. A professional will have the file date, iteration number and other facts imbedded with each proof.

A key advantage of digitally printing an edition is that all of the prints do not have to be made at the same time. However, it is very important that a BAT be kept by the printmaker so that every print that is made in the future can be compared to the approved proof. This is important because so many variables exist in a digital printing workflow that if the tenth print in an edition is produced six months later, it may not match the first print. Issues with the file, the printer, or the media can all affect the color. For example, the file may be corrupted or improperly saved (e.g. the wrong size or iteration). It is possible for the performance of the printer to be affected by recent repairs, relocation, updates, operator error, or temperature, or humidity changes that affect how the ink flows through the nozzles. The media may also be affected by changes in temperature and humidity or a new batch made with a slightly different chemistry in the ink-receptive coating. Color may also be compromised if the media profile has been altered in any way.

An experienced printmaker can bring all of these variables back into alignment before printing a reorder but only if a BAT is on hand for comparison. A simple comparison between the archived BAT and a new test strip that has been specifically created prior to any reorder can prevent lost time, waste, and disappointment. Do not expect to proof reorders, it is the responsibility of the printer to adhere to the aforementioned steps.

Not all printmakers make BATs. But unless you plan to print your entire edition at the same time without any possibility of future reprints, the creation of a BAT is an important discussion to have with your printmaker.

5

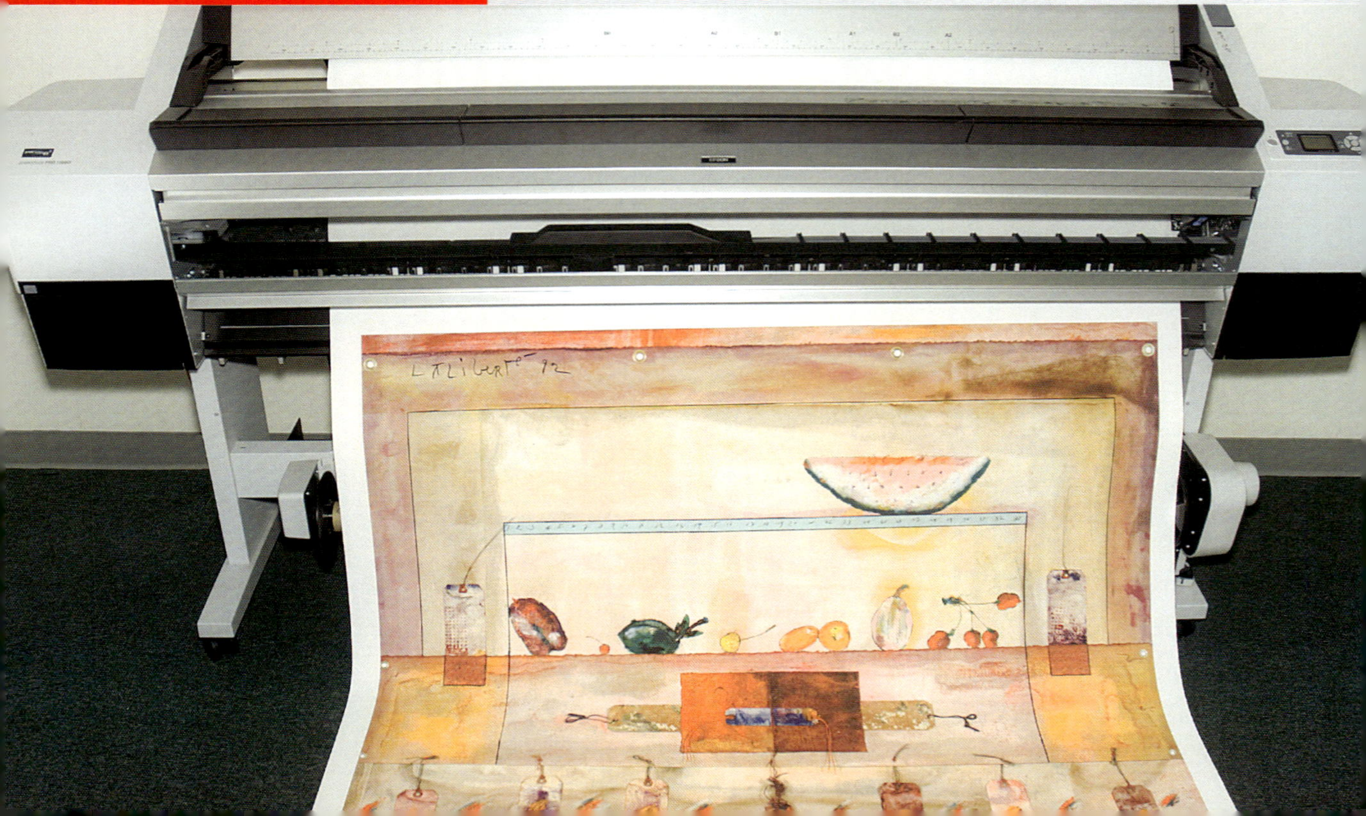

The Print

The digital capture is complete and the resulting file has been proofed and approved. Now it is time to print, and a whole new set of decisions awaits you. Some of these include choices about the print substrate (referred to as "media"), print size, and finishing options that are best suited for your work.

Although there are dozens of makes and models of printers on the market, only a few models are appropriate for creating quality digital fine art reproductions. Unless you understand a few basic facts about these state-of-the-art printers for art reproduction, your best bet is to find the most skilled and experienced printmaker possible, and leave it up to him to use the make and model printer he prefers.

State-of-the-Art Printers

Inkjet printing technology for fine-art reproduction has developed rapidly over the past 15 years.

For the purposes of this book, all you need to know is whether the printmaker you select is using a state-of-the-art, high resolution, wide gamut, pigment ink printer. Ranging from twenty-four inches to sixty four inches wide, these are the printers most commonly used to reproduce limited editions of art that will remain stable.

To reiterate, while the quality of the printer is vital, the ability to make a quality reproduction does not reside solely within the printer itself. Rather, the results depends on a proper file, the printmaker's equipment, experience, expertise, and talent. The printmaker's ability to communicate well his willingness to build a strong working relationship with you are also necessary to make the whole reproduction process work to your satisfaction.

Types of Inks Used

The wide-format inkjet printers used to create the most detailed and precise reproductions use at least eight colors of environmentally friendly, water-based (aqueous) pigment inks. The current generation of Epson Stylus Pro printers use nine colors of ink with a highly advanced printhead that can vary the size of each ink droplet being ejected. Because the HP and Canon printers use thermal printheads that cannot vary the size of each ink droplet, they require more ink colors to create a color gamut that is more or less equal to that of the Stylus Pro.

Note that all of the professional model inkjet printers for art reproduction use pigment inks. Before creating so-called "giclée" prints at home, be sure that your desktop printer uses pigment inks. Many printers do not; they still use dye inks that will shift colors or fade within a few years. Some use solvent inks that are not environmentally safe or necessary to use.

Print Calibrations and Profiles

After the media has been selected, your printmaker must use the appropriate "profile." A profile is a computer code that controls how the printheads in a particular inkjet printer discharge each ink color for the substrate you have selected. A high-quality profile will determine whether or not you will get the best possible results from the combination of inks, print settings, and paper or canvas used with a given model of inkjet printer. Using the correct print profile with a calibrated monitor saves time and money because the printmaker can make color corrections that will print accurate proofs on the media you have selected.

Creating print profiles can be time-consuming. Some printmakers download profiles provided either by the manufacturer of the printer or the media supplier. The profiles are "generic" because they are designed to provide results that are "good-enough" for most models of printers operating in "typical" conditions.

The printmakers who are most serious about top-quality will use color-measuring devices to create their own "custom" profiles for each type of media they offer and the specific printer being used. A custom-made profile gives the printmaker ultimate control over the final print quality. Printmakers who have more than one printer will write a separate custom profile for every type of media they stock and for each printer. This is true even when more than one model of the same printer is used.

Creating custom profiles requires patience, technical know-how, a professional eye for color, and the "tools of the trade" that create and read color charts which the printmaker must then analyze and adjust.

The Basic Properties of Print Substrates (Media)

In the world of digital fine art printing, paper and canvas are collectively referred to as "media." The printmaker can select from a wealth of media types to offer artists for their reproductions. Rather than trying to source something yourself, it is best to choose your media from what the printmaker has to offer. That is because the printmaker has invested considerable time and money in researching the quality and performance of different materials particularly with regards to their ability to reproduce color.

Inkjet Receptive Coating:
One of the leading quality indicators of media is not readily seen with the naked eye. It is the microscopically thin inkjet receptive coating that is applied to the surface of an art paper or canvas. The purpose of this coating is to control how precisely the droplets of pigment ink spread and form color. The coatings also affect how much total ink the media can hold, how quickly the prints dry, and how well the print resists smearing and smudging. All inkjet media—whether it's paper, canvas, or a specialty surface such as metal—must have an inkjet-receptive coating. The coating will also provide for an extended lifespan.

Some of the best papers and canvases for digital fine art printing are made by the same companies that manufacture some of the materials you use to create your originals. The reason is simple: they already make products for artists and understand the type of quality you expect. However, the companies that manufacture art papers and canvas must still have their products custom coated for inkjet art reproduction. In most cases, this coating is performed by another company. If the coating process isn't done properly or consistently, the final print results become problematic. Thus, the overall performance of the digital fine art media may not produce the same level of quality as the brand of uncoated paper or canvas you choose for your original work.

A qualified digital fine art printmaker will offer only those media that they know from experience will provide great results. An experienced printmaker also pays attention to ongoing advances in media and will test new products introduced to the market that offer new distinctions such as those made from sustainable resources. Unfortunately, some printmakers continue to use some of the early inkjet media even though these materials have proven to be less "archival" than originally believed and do not perform as well as newer products. An experienced printmaker will also be knowledgeable about the type of media that works best for reproducing a particular piece of art.

Rolls or Sheets:

Digital media comes in sheets and rolls and most wide-format inkjet printers can accommodate both types. Sheets typically come in a variety of standard paper sizes from 8 x 10 up to 36 x 48. Rolls of media may be anywhere from twenty-four to sixty inches wide and up to fifty feet long.

Printing on rolls is often more cost effective because you can make one very large print or several of other sizes without having to stop the printer to reload.

Archival Properties:

If you look up the word archival in a dictionary, you will not find a number associated with its definition. Archival is not a technical term. Rather, it is an adjective that relates to whether or not something is suitable for archiving. It only suggests that certain items (or their components) are durable and chemically stable. In other words; will the material age well? No one can guarantee for sure how long a certain material will last. The phrase "archival for x number of years" is not quantifiable despite how rigorously it has been "tested." Nor does the term "acid free" promise that the paper will archive well. Longevity can be affected by buffers and neutralizing acids as well as uncontrolled conditions in the environment in which the print is displayed.

The digital printing process involves the interaction of many elements each with their own chemical make-up. For example, the base material, the inkjet receptive coating, the inks, and any applied protective coatings all can affect how long a print will remain stable (e.g. without fading or discoloration).

How the paper is manufactured can also make a difference. Although whiter papers can appear brighter, many extra-white papers are manufactured with optical brighteners (OB's), some formulations of which may have affected the archival properties of the paper. The use of some types of OB's in fine art media (and in canvas coatings) may make the media less archival than those that contain measurably fewer or no OB's.

While different media manufacturers will produce all sorts of scientific tests and data to support their claims against competing products, newer and more advanced product chemistries are being developed all the time making previous studies irrelevant. So, once again, it is best to rely on a good printmaker for recommendations.

Consider also that the possible combinations of inks, coating chemistries, and papers are nearly limitless; so coming to a final conclusion about the projected lifespan of a print can be difficult, if not impossible. Thus, many media manufacturers no longer make any "archival" claims. If you like doing research into how prints are tested for permanence, there are some good sources of information available. While most are focused on photographic prints, some publications explain in clear, basic language some of the factors that affect inkjet print permanence and the limitations and drawbacks of predictive testing. On the other hand, if you are like most artists, you simply want to get back to work in your studio and rely on an experienced digital fine art printmaker with a good reputation to guide you.

FIG. 5.1 — PAPER PRINTING MEDIA OPTIONS

MEDIA	SURFACE	SUGGESTIONS FOR REPRODUCING
Hot Press	smooth (no texture)	Work on Canvas* (or board). Work on Paper (oil, acrylic, pastel, charcoal, color pencil, graphite, mixed media).
Cold Press	"watercolor" texture	Watercolors
Etching	subtle, even texture	Pastels, charcoals, fine art prints

Will not compete with printed canvas texture.

While it is not that common, when there is a legitimate reason to coat paper, this additional step can be effective, but will probably add to the cost. Proper profiling, color management techniques, and the correct paper for the job should be fully explored first, so that coating a matte paper is not used as a quick fix.

FIG. 5.2 — CANVAS PRINTING MEDIA OPTIONS

MEDIA	SURFACE	CONTENT DESCRIPTIONS
100% Cotton	matte*, medium texture	Natural cotton fibers may cause surface irregularities. These irregularities often are small raised nubs which can be noticeable in places that are distracting to the art.
Cotton/ Poly Blend	matte*, medium texture	The blend provides a more even surface; at times, irregularities can exist from the cotton content, but it is rarely a problem.
Cotton/ Poly Blend Pre-finsihed	satin or gloss medium texture	Same as Cotton/Poly above, but with a factory applied finish on which the final image is printed.

Prints require coating

A coating must be applied to all prints created on matte canvas to add a reflective surface to the finished print, as well as some additional UV protection and durability. Make sure the coating has been applied to the strips when approving proofs on matte canvas.

Choosing the Right Print Media

Choosing the right type of media for your reproduction is similar to choosing the surface that is most appropriate before starting your original. In most cases, you will want your reproduction to closely match the look of your original. However, there may be times when you want to create reproductions on surfaces that are a bit different than the surface on which you created your original. The choice is all yours, but do your homework.

Before hiring a printmaker to reproduce your art, find out what types of media he offers and how knowledgeable he is about each product. For the purpose of this book, it would be impossible to list all the media currently available for digital fine art reproduction. Following are some tips and questions to ask to help with your decision-making process.

Ask to see the sample book:
A good printmaker should have a book (such as a binder) with paper samples that can be removed, handled, and compared side by side. Look carefully at the selection, and when you inspect them side-by-side, compare nuances such as the variations in surface texture and paper color.

Take into account your palette:
Ask the printmaker to recommend which paper would perform best with your type of work. For example, if your art has a lot of dark colors, your printmaker may recommend one paper over another simply because it is better at reproducing dark colors.

Consider how the underlying tone and texture will affect your print:
The tone of the paper can be another important consideration when going through the selection process. If you have intentionally left white space in your watercolor painting, you may want to select a digital fine art paper that has the same tone and texture as your original. In this case, you will want to compare the paper sample with the paper used for your original artwork. If you have densely applied paints to the surface of your original, you do not need to be as concerned about the "tone" of the underlying print media, but you will still want to consider the texture.

Matte paper choices are varied:
As you can see, for the most part, there are no hard-and-fast rules. You may have a reason to select a paper surface other than that on which your original was created. Much of the selection process is a balance between performance, appropriateness, likes, and dislikes. Usually, the correct choice for the project becomes clear after you make some observations and comparisons. (See fig 5.1: Paper Media Options.) Digital gloss papers should not be used for reproducing paintings. These are typically used for photographic printing. Artists who have experimented with printing fine art on gloss surfaces have found that these prints are typically not accepted by the art world. Additionally, these papers tend to include synthetic materials that give them their glossy finish. In certain circumstances they ripple once framed.

Choosing the right canvas:
The canvas selection process is more straightforward than choosing the right paper. This is because neither a truly rough textured canvas nor a truly smooth canvas currently exists for digital fine art printing. Most are very similar in texture.

If you paint without a lot of texture or work on surfaces such as masonite, you may want to choose either a hot-press digital fine-art paper or accept the surface change of current digital fine art canvases. (See fig. 5.2: Canvas Media Options).

It has become the norm to print on canvas when reproducing an original that was executed on canvas. Although quality reproductions of oil or acrylic paintings may be made on paper, the print will often look different than the original since the paper has a matte finish instead of the glossier finish of a canvas.

It is also important to understand that paintings not painted on canvas will experience a surface change when printed on canvas. The lack of canvas texture in the original will be altered by the canvas texture (of the media being printed on). Ultimately, you must use your own aesthetic judgment about the print and whether or not it conveys the results you had in mind. Artists often choose to make reproductions on surfaces different from the original work. But when you're doing it for the first time, look carefully at your proofs before making a final decision.

There may be times when it feels as if more than one media is worth further consideration. An experienced printmaker will understand your concerns and be willing to provide pricing for proofing on more than one media. It is most practical to run an additional proof on a second media only after the color has been approved on the first media. If the printmaker has done a good job of setting up their color management systems ("profiling"), creating additional proofs should not require a lot of work.

Specialty Surfaces

One of the great advantages of digital fine art reproduction is that you can experiment with printing your work on an increasing number of other surfaces, including fabrics, metals, and rice papers.

Generally, there are two categories of specialty media: those that must be coated by hand before printing and those materials to which an inkjet receptive coating has already been applied by the same companies that coat art papers and canvases. Some substrates designed for signage can offer additional options and effects but should never be used for prints that are meant for anything other than short-term use. (See fig 5.3: Specialty Media Options)

Hand applied coatings:
An inkjet printing coating can be hand applied to almost any type of material on which you want to print. However, the thickness of the substrate must be taken into consideration because the printmaker does not want to risk damaging the printheads on the printer. Hand applied coatings can incur more expense since each piece (even those used for proofing) must be prepared. To learn more about the possibilities and costs, speak with an experienced fine art printmaker.

Pre coated materials:
The good news is that a variety of specialty materials with pre-applied coatings is on the rise. This may make it more feasible for more artists to try making reproductions on non-traditional materials in the future.

For example, individuals have been experimenting with a variety of printing methods on different types of metals. If the metal is thin enough, a coating may be applied by hand. For thicker metals, the art may be printed on a film first and then transferred to the surface of the metal. Nowadays, metals of appropriate thickness are available that have been prepared in advance for fine art inkjet printing. In this case there is no preparation or transfer step; the metal goes directly through the printer like any other media.

There are all kinds of reasons to pick one method or product over another. The decision should stem from your aesthetic goals and the parameters of the project. Once again, an experienced printmaker is your best resource.

FIG. 5.3 — SPECIALTY PRINTING MEDIA OPTIONS		
MEDIA	**SURFACE**	**PRINTING SUGGESTIONS**
Wall/ Mural Paper	smooth	Paste and hang as any other wall paper. Perfect for murals.
Rice Paper	available in a variety of colors and textures	Watercolor, calligraphy, art that will work well with the unique surface quality.
Metal	smooth, matte, brushed or shinny, in a variety of metallic colors	Virtually any art can be experimented with for printing on metal, including mixed media, oil paintings and digital art images. Note limitations concerning size and/or thickness need to be considered.
Silky, poly, cotton blends	various, mostly semi-transparent	Suitable for fine art for short term use, such as part of an installation. Not archival, yellowing or fading may occur. Other forms of printing should be explored.
Other	vinyl and plastics	See above. Mostly used for outdoor or indoor show signage.

Choosing Your Print Size

One key advantage of digital fine art reproduction is that it gives you a tremendous range of choices in terms of print sizes. Because it does not require the use of printing plates, you could conceivably make your reproductions any number of different sizes, but even so, you really want to have a plan.

When asked about print sizes, my advice is always the same: Limit the selection of image sizes. It is good to have some variety, but it is better to make a few sensible choices. Having a limited selection of sizes is important because keeping track of too many size variations can be confusing. Offering too many print sizes can also adversely affect sales. The average buyer is easily sidetracked and can even become confused by too many options. This can lead to loosing the sale.

Do not feel obligated to fulfill everyone's requests. Before agreeing to make a custom-size print, qualify the buyer to be sure it will be worth your time to do so. If you know the person, and they have purchased from you before, then it is probably best to accommodate the request. But check that the size they are requesting is proportional to your original before making any promises or quoting a price.

Remember: You are the professional. Trust the decisions you make about your print collection. If you feel inclined not to get involved with custom-size prints, that is your prerogative. If you make this choice from the start, you will be better equipped to respond professionally when asked about custom sizes. You will also be prepared to make alternative suggestions. When determining your size offerings, there are some other factors to take into consideration.

Same Size Prints:
One of the most frequently asked questions is: "Should I make prints the same size as my original?" There is no single best way to answer this, because a lot depends on the nature of your work and your plans for the reproductions. Often, the question about printing at actual size comes from a larger concern about how it will compete with or affect the value of the original. Throughout history there has been no evidence of this being a problem. Consider this: an original will maintain its value and there will always be buyers who only want the original. Considerations also include the size of your originals; if they are not too large, you may not want to reduce them any further. If they are very large, offering smaller sizes can lead to more sales. Ultimately, it is a personal decision, so do what makes you comfortable. From experience, I can tell you that the majority of digital reproduction prints differ in size from the original artwork. Many artists choose to print their work "one size smaller" which usually works out to be about two-thirds the size of the original. Using stock frame sizes and offering another price point are two reasons artists may choose to reduce the size of their original artwork.

Stock Frame Sizing:
It is very common for artists to ask for print sizes that will fit into stock frame sizes. This can save a lot of money in terms of framing costs, but do not allow your aesthetic decisions as an artist be dictated by stock frame sizes. Ultimately, it is far more important to respect the artistic integrity of the original and your intentions as an artist. In some cases, you can "crop" your image to make it fit a standard stock frame size. But crop your image only if it will save you money and does not greatly alter the image as a whole.

Reducing and Enlarging Your Image:

What size is appropriate for the work being reproduced? When using a printmaker with the ability to create very high-resolution files, the possibilities are extensive. With good resolution and perfect focus during the capture stage, images can technically be made larger without any trouble.

What you need to consider before having your image enlarged by 50% or more is how the enlargement will affect the appearance of the applied art medium. For example, if art is enlarged 100%, a one inch brushstroke will become two inches. I have worked with artists who plan for this change and consider their final print to be more indicative of the look they are going for. When reducing an image, the scale of the applied medium will also change, by becoming incrementally smaller. In either case, be sure to check a proof at the new size before making a final decision.

It is also a good idea to think about how the print size will affect the selling price. If you decide that a small print is appropriate for your work, think about some of the reasons you would want to make smaller images. For example, the most common reason to make smaller prints is to be able to offer another price point to buyers. If that is one of your goals, then be sure to evaluate whether the cost of producing the smaller print is going to allow you to sell it at a price that will leave you with an acceptable profit. While "ganging" up smaller prints across a wide roll of media may bring down the unit costs, there are other situations in which the reverse can happen. For example, the wider the roll, the more the media costs, so producing certain sizes of smaller prints can actually increase the net cost of each print. Again, this is where your printmaker's guidance is really important. Working with a printmaker who is capable of addressing marketing strategies is most helpful. At the very least, ask your printmaker to supply pricing for a variety of sizes and print quantities so you can identify where the price breaks work in your advantage.

There are a couple of other factors to consider regarding the size of prints as well. Small prints usually have minimum order requirements. You should also think about the psychology that often goes along with making a purchase. Perceived value is very real in terms of its affect on sales, so consider how the buyer may view the size of your reproduction versus its price. In most cases, the perceived value of a large print may be greater than small prints. In any case, being true to the art and knowing the demographics of your target market will help guide you. Offering a variety of sizes at different price points is best achieved by printing the sizes that are most artistically appropriate for each original. Over time, the mix of your prints collectively will provide buyers with a nice range of sizes and prices.

Completing the Final Print

Before the final print is run, more decisions need to be made. You need to think about how the final print will be framed, trimmed, coated, and packed. A qualified printmaker should offer all these postprint services: trimming, coating, stretching, and wrapping.

Trimming Prints on Paper:
Paper prints come out of the printer ready to be trimmed and packed. Typically they are trimmed to the image size plus margins. Margin options are ultimately up to you based partly on how you plan to sell or frame the prints.

The bullet points below list the three most common options for margins. Keep in mind that margin size probably will affect the price per print, so make sure you understand the price differences before making a final decision.

- **One inch on all four sides:** Offering narrower margins is up to the printmaker; although, artists selling unframed prints may want to consider the general appearance of the final print and request a wider margin. Margins that are too skimpy can make your print look cheap and less professional. If you are planning on selling your prints matted or framed, the one inch margin is all you need and it will save you money.

- **Two inches or more on all four sides:**
  Prints larger than 16 x 20 look nicer with a
  wider margin, unless they are going to be
  framed before showing or selling. There
  are no rules regarding this, but it is worth
  thinking about. Some artists will opt for
  2.5 inch or 3 inch margins. If you plan to
  sell unframed prints (or wish to keep your
  options open), then remember, as the
  print gets larger, so should the margin.

- **Weighted Bottom:** When the bottom
  margin is larger than an equal margin used
  on the other three sides, it is referred to as
  a weighted margin. The main reason for
  considering this trimming option is that it
  provides a larger, more distinctive area for
  signing, titling, and numbering. It can also
  offer some "added value" selling options as
  discussed later in Chapter 8.

Finishing Prints on Canvas:

Unlike prints on paper, the canvas print requires
a number of additional steps before it is ready
for delivery. These steps include applying a
clear protective coating (unless printing on a
pre-coated canvas) and stretching the canvas
on the same stretcher bars typically used on
your original.

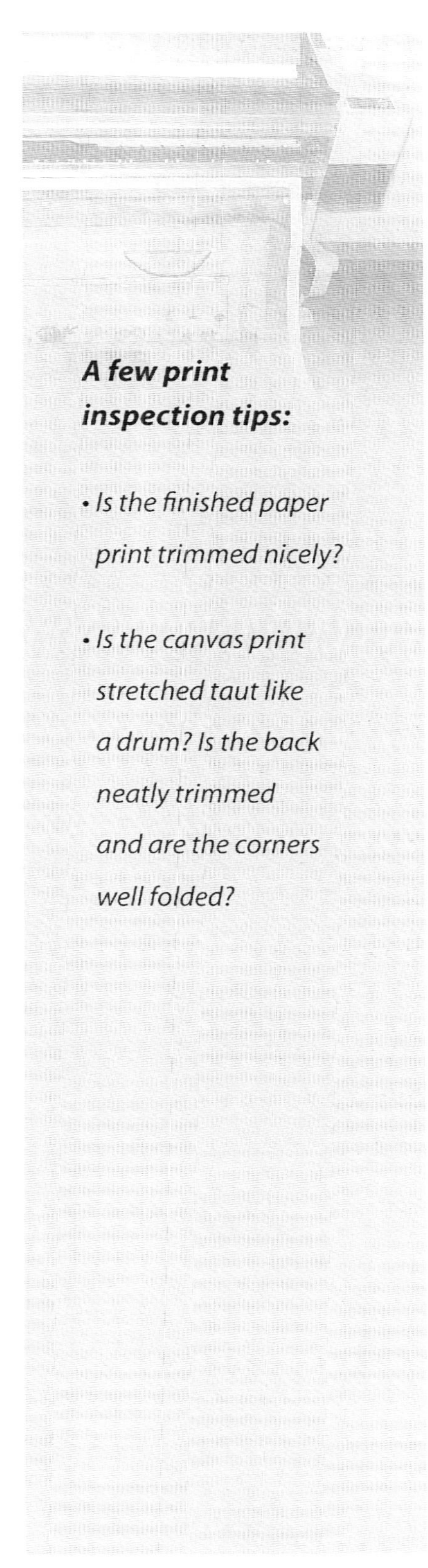

**A few print
inspection tips:**

• Is the finished paper
  print trimmed nicely?

• Is the canvas print
  stretched taut like
  a drum? Is the back
  neatly trimmed
  and are the corners
  well folded?

A choice you will need to make at this stage is the surface finish of the protective coating. Digital fine art coatings available are matte, satin, semi-gloss, and gloss. Selecting which to use is often best decided based upon the finish of the original art. The vast majority of canvas prints are finished off with a semi-gloss coating.

Before a canvas print can be coated, it must first be hung for "outgassing." This step is necessary to keep the coated print surface from becoming cloudy later. After a print has outgassed for at least 24 hours, the print is ready to coat with a formula specially made and thoroughly tested for use with aqueous inkjet inks. These coatings will make the surface more durable while also providing some additional protection against the fading caused by UV light.

Different printmakers use different methods of coating depending on how their facility is set up or on their personal preferences. Some may use a spray booth while others may hand-apply the coating with a brush or roller. Typically, two coats are applied allowing at least four hours or more between coats according to atmospheric conditions. Whatever application method is used, the coating should appear smooth and even across the entire surface of the print.

Never accept an uncoated canvas print unless it was printed on pre coated canvas. Pre coated canvases have a satin or glossy coating applied by the canvas manufacturer. The printmaker then prints over the coated surface. The final look of this is distinctively different than post print coating methods and is more often used for mass reproduction. I am often asked whether it is a good idea to coat the canvas with the varnishes artists use on their original paintings. This is not a good idea because you cannot be sure that the varnish or coating you want to use will be compatible with the properties of the digital inks and media. When the coating is thoroughly dry, the next and final step for the canvas print is the stretching. Here once again there are choices to be made.

The printmaker should offer a variety of stretching options. Each option will require leaving appropriate margin sizes for the style planned for your print. Expect to pay more for canvas prints that will be used with thicker heavy-duty stretcher bars. Not only will the bars themselves cost more, but the print itself will require more canvas in order to accommodate the wider margins. (See fig 5.4: Canvas Stretching Options.) The final stretched canvas should be taut and placed properly on the stretcher bar frame.

Mounting is another option for finishing a canvas print. Artists can choose to trim the print to the image and adhere the canvas to board or other substrates.

FIG 5.4 — CANVAS PRINT STRETCHING OPTIONS

	BAR THICKNESS	SIDE COLOR	STAPLES	RECOMMENDED FOR
Standard wrap white sides	3/4"	white	side	Paintings to be framed.
Standard wrap color margins	3/4"	complimentary color	back	Ideal for offering the option to frame or hang as is.
Gallery wrap color margins	1.5"*	complimentary color	back	More contemporary, ready for hanging.
Gallery wrap mirrored image	1.5"*	image is cloned for use on the sides	back	More contemporary, ready for hanging.

** 1.5" stretcher bars are considered heavy duty. Medium weight, 1.25" bars also exist and can be useful for eliminating the weight of gallery wrapped large pieces.*

Packing, Shipping, and Storing Prints

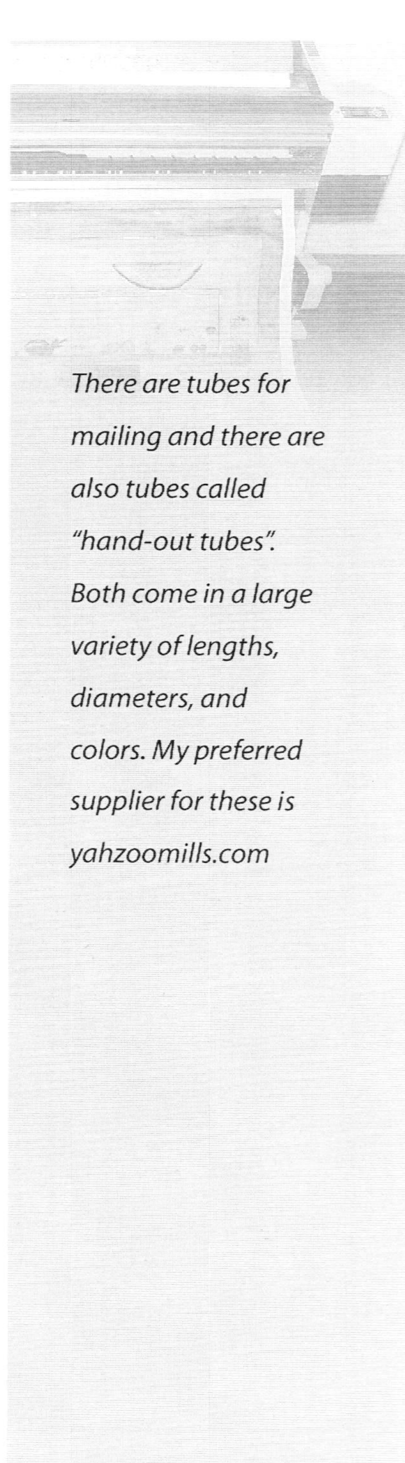

There are tubes for mailing and there are also tubes called "hand-out tubes". Both come in a large variety of lengths, diameters, and colors. My preferred supplier for these is yahzoomills.com

Prints on Paper:

A professional printmaker will exercise great care in packing and shipping prints. As an artist, you should be aware of some of these methods.

Packing Paper Prints:

Insert rolled prints into rigid mailing tubes that are at least three inches in diameter and two inches longer than the length of the rolled print. When rolling paper prints, do not roll them tightly, and avoid using force. Use acid-free paper to protect the rolled print. Use small pieces of tape to secure the paper to the rolled print to keep the print itself from unrolling.

To make it easier, roll the print around a smaller diameter tube in a manner that ensures that the smaller tube can easily slide out after the print has been rolled and the acid-free paper has been taped around the rolled print. If you plan to pack more than one print in the same tube, use a mailing tube with an appropriate diameter.

Packing Flat Prints:

Prints that are going to be packaged flat may need to go through a "D-Roller" first. A D-Roller is a device designed to remove any "curl memory" that may remain when prints are produced on rolls.

Flat prints may be packed individually or in bulk. Some printmakers may offer individual packaging as part of their standard services but at an additional cost that is usually based upon print size. When prints will be packed individually, each print should be inserted into a crystal-clear cellophane bag along with a rigid, acid-free backer such as an archival foam-core board. The packaging presents the image well when you sell unframed prints. Not only are they ready for display in a print rack, but they are also prepared for delivery to the print buyer.

Shipping:

After the rolled print is inserted into the mailing tube, simply add plastic end caps secured with packing tape. This keeps the prints from being damaged and discourages pilfering during shipping.

Flat prints require more work to ship, but the extra effort is worth it because it is best if paper prints remain flat. First, pack prints as previously described, then wrap them in a layer of bubble wrap making them one complete package. This will keep the prints from sliding around inside the box. Next, select a box that is at least two inches larger per side than the packaged print(s). The box should also be deep enough to include additional protection to the top and bottom. Before placing the packed prints into the carton, create a bed of packing peanuts on the bottom. After putting the prints on the bed of peanuts, fill the remaining space with more peanuts and tape all of the box seams.

Prints on Canvas:

Packing and shipping canvas prints is a bit easier than packing prints on paper because of the nature of the canvas itself. The only rule to remember is to never ship canvas prints that have not been treated with a protective coating. The coating must be completely dry before the prints are packed and shipped.

Packing Rolled:

Rolling unstretched prints is the ideal way to ship very large prints on canvas. Use the same techniques described above when rolling unstretched prints. However, because prints on canvas are easier to roll and less fragile, you probably will not need to roll the print around a smaller diameter tube.

Packing Flat:

When you pick up your canvas prints from the printmaker, each print should be neatly wrapped in a cello bag. Some large canvases may require more than one bag to be fashioned into a suitable covering, but the overall packing should appear neat and tidy.

Shipping:

Stretched canvases should be individually packed in cello bags and then stacked front-to-front in bubble wrap. Once this is done, the steps for packing the prints into a shipping carton is much the same as described for shipping flat paper prints.

I prefer stacking stretched canvases flat rather than packing them upright in a row. Stacking them flat allows the prints to float safely in a cloud of peanuts and better withstand damage to the outer carton.

Storing Prints:

Whether the unframed prints are wrapped in cello bags or unwrapped, prints on paper should always be stored flat and ideally in metal flat files designed for holding art. If metal flat files are not available, prints should be stored flat in a place where they are protected from heat and direct sunlight. Any prints that are wrapped with packaging materials that are not acid-free should be unwrapped before they are stored.

Just like original art on canvas, prints on canvas should be stored in vertical canvas files on their longest edge to avoid warping. The storage space should have some air flow. Canvas prints should be stored back-to-back if they are unframed and have no hanging hardware. If the prints have hanging hardware, place them face to face.

In areas that are susceptible to frequent changes in temperature and humidity, it is best to store prints unwrapped.

Framing Prints

Fine art reproductions should be handled with the same care as original art. Never mount prints, period! Mounting techniques and materials can often cause problems such as yellowing or surface damage.

Prints on paper are safest when attached to an acid-free backer using framer's hinging tape and then matted with an acid-free mat for a professional look. Prints on canvas should be stretched or mounted to wood using archival paste or glue.

When framing prints to show and/or sell, it is important to strike the right balance between cost and appearance. Although this can pose a real challenge, it is smart to select a frame that is both cost effective and appropriate for the art style, palette, and subject matter.

To manage your frame costs, create a good working relationship with a local retailer. You can also make bulk purchases online. You may also try shopping in some of the large art supply and craft stores where you can find some very decent standard frames at amazing prices. Watch for sales!

Framing Prints on Paper:
Consider the type of glass that will be used. Because a qualified printmaker should be providing "archival-quality" prints, there is no need to buy museum glass. This will only add extra cost to your reproductions. When selecting mats, there are two things I recommend. The most important of these is using archival mats only. While others may be less expensive, the damage they can cause to a print over an unpredictable length of time is not worth the savings. The other recommendation is to stay with neutral colors when choosing a mat. The sale of a print can be lost when it is framed with a colored matte. It is generally less professional and it may present a problem for the buyer's decor. Also, avoid non glare glass and plexiglass because they are not always the best choice aesthetically and some may inflate the price. (The only exception would be if you are supplying art for healthcare facilities or other public spaces that require the use of nonbreakable framing materials).

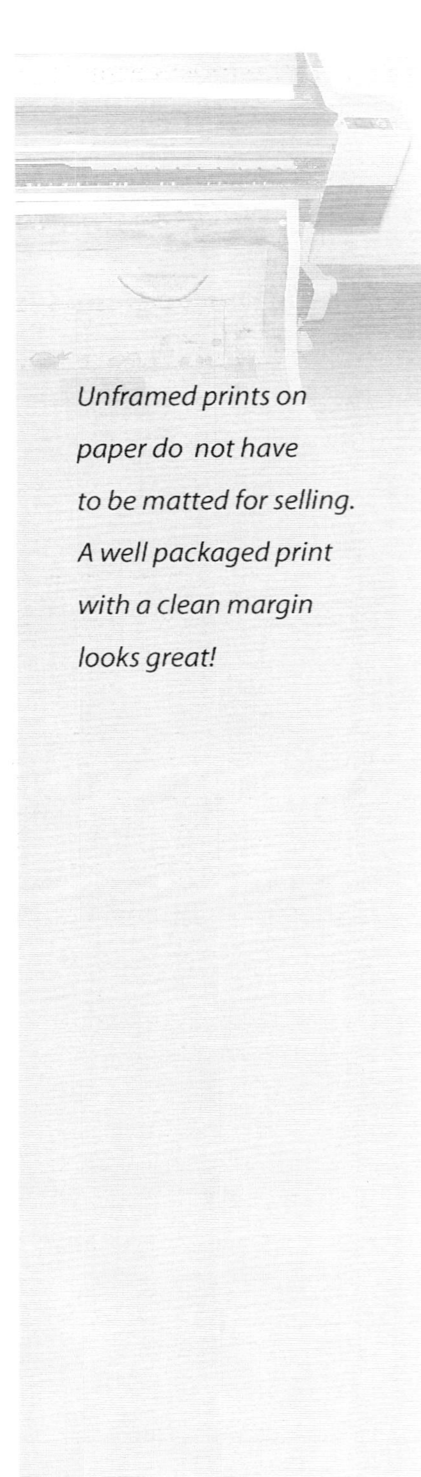

Framing Prints on Canvas:

Gallery wrapped prints do not require framing because the edges of the stretcher bars are completely hidden by wrapping the printed canvas around all four sides. Not all images are appropriate for gallery wrapping and may be better off framed. However, if appropriate, this style of finishing a canvas print is growing in popularity. There is added cost to ordering gallery wrapped prints from the printmaker, but it eliminates the cost of framing. For canvas prints that are to be framed, the rules are pretty much the same as those for paper prints, except there is no mat involved.

Some additional factors should be considered when planning canvas print sizes. For canvas prints, avoid print sizes that include fractions because that will require the added expense of custom-made stretcher bars. Odd number sizes can also be problematic when using heavy duty stretcher bars since they are most commonly available in whole sizes only.

The following chart includes examples of sizes that provide the most versatile proportions. The reasons for being familiar with these sizes are: 1) their ability to proportion well for printing larger or smaller image sizes 2) they fit stock frames and 3) for cost effective printing. This applies to prints on paper or canvas. However, there are some additional factors when planning canvas print sizes. For those it is helpful to avoid sizes that contain fractions since they will require custom made stretcher bars. Odd number sizes can be problematic when using heavy duty stretcher bars since they are most commonly available in whole sizes only.

FIG. 5.5 — IMAGE SIZES THAT PROPORTION WELL		
SAMPLE SIZE	**SMALLER PROPORTIONS(S)**	**LARGER PROPORTION(S)**
24" x 32"	18" x 24"	30" x 40"
20" x 30"	16" x 24"	24" x 36"
16" x 20"	8" x 10"	24" x 30"

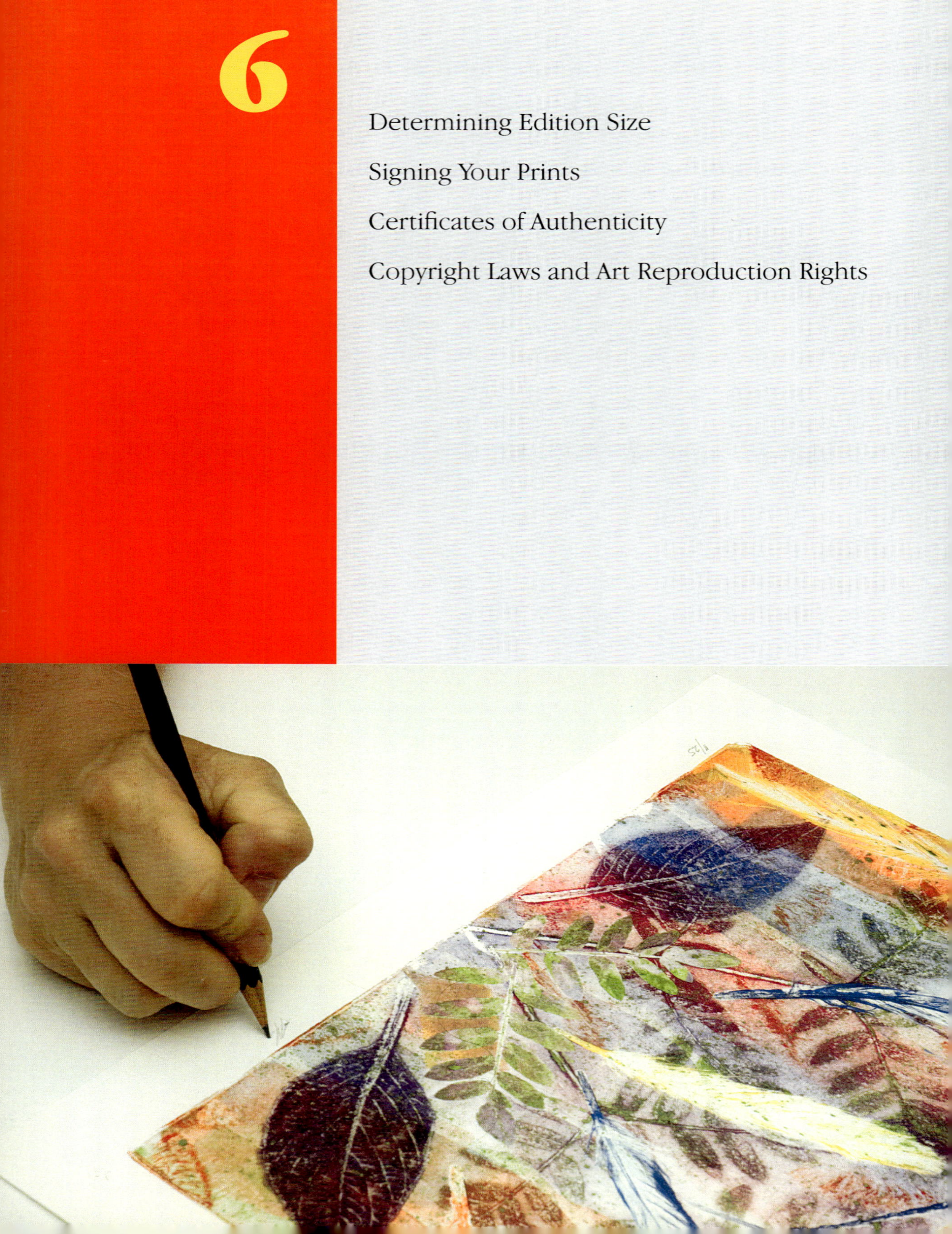

6

Edition Sizes, Signatures, and Other Final Steps

The rapid rise of digital fine art reproduction has raised a number of questions with regards to: the size of an edition, whether prints need to be numbered, and how prints should be signed. Because there are no formal guidelines or standards, a lot will depend on your goals as an artist and how you want to be perceived in the art market. In some ways, the art market is at a crossroads between the traditions that served artists and buyers well in the past and the need to adopt new ways of thinking in light of the capabilities associated with digital methods of reproducing fine art.

Determining Edition Size

If your goal is to build awareness of your work and provide a revenue source to supplement the sale of your originals, you may want to take advantage of the flexibility now available when selecting the size of your edition.

The practice of numbering prints began long ago with some of the fine art reproduction techniques we discussed in Chapter 2 (e.g., etchings, chromolithography, etc.). The underlying rationale of numbered editions was partly to identify which prints came off the readied surface (plate, stone, etc.) first, second, and so on. It was typically thought that the first prints after any artist's proofs (A/P) of an edition were the best and most valuable. Traditionally, the size of the edition was determined by the performance of the plate. The plates used in traditional printmaking processes wore down as the edition number increased affecting the quality or appearance of the later prints until the plate was destroyed. Once the chosen edition size was reached or the printing surface failed to satisfy the artist's expectations, the edition was complete.

Plates used in commercial offset lithography are designed to accurately and consistently reproduce thousands of copies of an original. Because the cost of setting up and running a job on a commercial printing press can be high, editions created with offset lithography typically are between two hundred-fifty and one-thousand prints. Because digital printing does not use any plates, there is no technical reason that the 100th print in an edition should look the least bit different from the very first print in an edition. You may be wondering why we continue to number reproduced editions if the technical barriers to consistent production of high-quality prints have disappeared. The answer is simple: It is all about marketing. As long as many buyers and collectors of art continue to expect an edition to be numbered, it is best to stay the course. A reputable artist today would be wise not to charge more for the lower edition numbers.

Another aspect of digital fine art reproduction that affects edition sizes is the fact that not all of the prints in an edition have to be printed at the same time (as with commercial offset lithography). You do not have to commit to large print runs because additional prints can be ordered whenever you need them. This means that artists at all stages of their careers can afford to print editions and can set the edition size based upon other decisions. For example, a smaller edition has more perceived value, so which would you prefer: to sell hundreds of copies of a lower price print or fewer of a much higher price print?

You can choose to set an edition size in advance, but only make the actual prints as they are needed. When the last print in that edition is created, the edition is closed. If one of your images turns out to be more popular than you imagined and the edition sells out, you can create a new edition of the same image in another size or if appropriate, on a different type of media. Each size or media change is by law a new edition. (See fig. 6.1: Print Size Edition Options)

FIG 6.1 — EDITION SIZE OPTIONS

EDITION TYPE	EXAMPLE	ADVANTAGES	DISADVANTAGES
Signed Limited Edition	1/50	Perceived as more valuable.	May run out with more buyers wanting it.
Signed Un-numbered Edition	Edition of 50	Considered by some as easier to manage.	Less understood by buyers.
Signed Open Edition	O/E	No limit to how many can be available to sell.	Considered less valuable.
Artists Proof	A/P	Provides an opportunity to sell test prints.	None as long as AP prints are of acceptable quality.

Signing Your Prints

There are no clearly established guidelines or formal rules for properly signing digital fine art print reproductions. Once again, this creates questions that only you can answer, ideally with guidance from an experienced printmaker. For example, is it preferred to reproduce the painting as is, complete with your signature, or should your signature be digitally removed during the file preparation stage so you can personally sign each print in the edition? Like so many questions that have arisen during the evolution of digital fine art reproduction, this issue seems to have resolved itself for now. Both methods are acceptable; it is a matter of personal preference.

Based upon my personal observations from coaching artists and working with sellers and buyers of art, I offer the following guidelines to use whether or not you are numbering your prints. If you are not sure which approach is best for you, make note of how other artists are signing their prints. Ultimately, it is a matter of which approach feels right to you.

Signing Paper Prints:
Following tradition, most artists seem to have settled on signing, numbering, and titling their prints in pencil on the bottom margin. However, it is not out of the question to select another way. For example, you can add the edition number next to the printed signature using an appropriate medium in a color that will suit the print and will be visible. This option allows the piece to be matted up to the image without any print margin.

Signing Canvas Prints:

A fine line permanent marker is suggested for signing canvas prints. Where you put the signature is up to you. Some artists will just add the edition number next to the printed signature on the front of the canvas. However, the trend that seems to have become the norm is signing the canvas print on the back even if the signature has already been printed on the face of the canvas as part of the reproduction itself. In this case, most artists place the following information on the top stretcher bar: signature, title, and edition size. However, if the canvas has not been trimmed to the edge of the stretcher bar, then the extra canvas overlap on the back of the stretcher bar may also be used. And, as often seen on original canvases, the information may be written in pencil on the back of the printed image.

Best Practices for All Types of Prints:

Only accomplished artists with a strong selling history should date their prints because these dated prints will increase in value as their careers continue. In my opinion, prints by less established artists should not be dated because prints that do not sell immediately may be perceived as old or unpopular if they remain in the market too long. This is something to consider if your printmaker requires you to start with a relatively high initial print order.

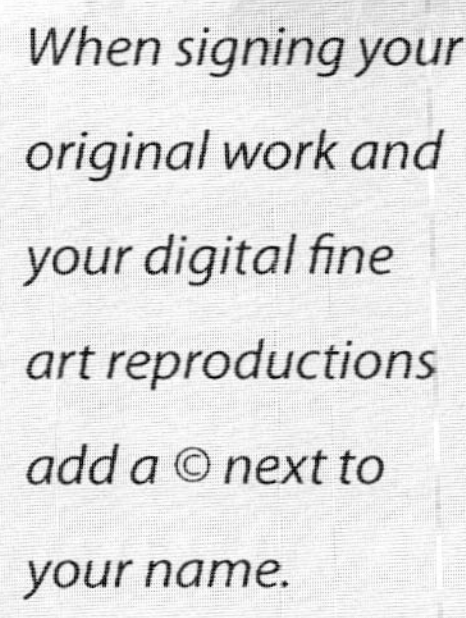

When signing your original work and your digital fine art reproductions add a © next to your name.

Find more about copyright in Chapter 7.

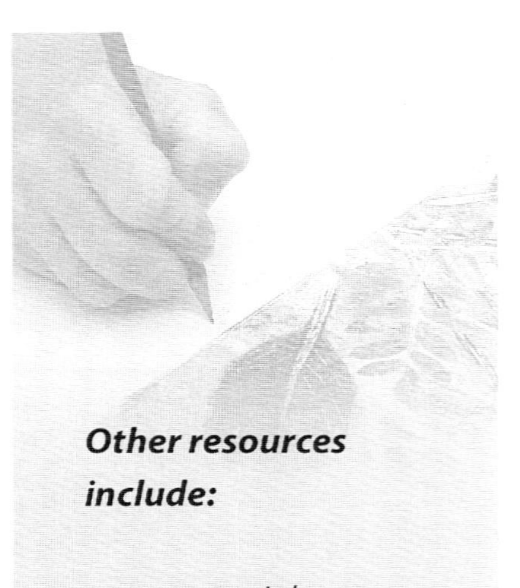

Certificates of Authenticity

Artists who wanted to provide some type of reassurance to members of the art-buying public frequently raised the issue of certificates of authenticity. Some printmakers offered a "certificate of authenticity" with each print. These certificates were usually computer generated and printed out on a desktop printer. Some were merely formatted on an 8.5 x 11 inch plain white page; others included a fancy border and the words "Certificate of Authenticity" in an equally fancy typeface to make the document look as official as possible. No official format existed, but most certificates included the artwork title, the edition size, and date, and were typically signed by both the artist and the printmaker. Since these were published by the printmaker and at times the artist, the resulting certificates were not much more than a piece of paper attempting to add credence to a print.

One paper company introduced a more professional looking version of a certificate that printmakers could purchase for their customers. The certificate was printed with a background similar in complexity and tone to that of currency. Later, they added an embedded silver strip much like on our dollar bills and a numbered, permanently adhered hologram seal. A companion holographic seal carrying the same number also accompanied each certificate. The second seal was to be affixed in the margins of the print. Despite these improvements in the certificates, the level of interest in authentication documentation diminished for a variety of reasons including the added cost per print. Over time, requests for certificates have markedly decresed.

My opinion is that if an artist signs and numbers the print, it has been authenticated! The artist's signature proves the domain, and the number certifies it as a print.

Replacing the certificate of authenticity with what I refer to as a "romance card" not only lends some authenticity, but it also adds provenance and is a nice selling tool. More about this is discussed in Chapter 7.

Copyright Laws and Art Reproduction Rights

Disclaimer: The following information is not legal advice. Legal rights can turn on specific facts or changes in the law. For specific advice, consult an attorney.

Copyright gives the artist the exclusive right to copy and distribute a work unless you have assigned it away or created the work as a W2 employee. A work automatically receives copyright protection once it becomes a tangible item; although, it needs to be registered with the United States Copyright Office before you can take legal action for an unauthorized use of your work.

Registration of Your Work:
It is best to apply common sense before jumping to register your work. Think about which of your works, if any, may be susceptible to misuse by another party. Ask yourself these questions: Does the work have some specific appeal to the mass market? Is it something unique or new? Has it been or will it be licensed for application to products? Will it have a lot of exposure? If you have answered "yes," to any of these questions, register your work and/ or seek legal counsel. The information to do so is easily found on www.copyright.gov.

Although registration is not required for copyright protection, registering your work does provide some advantages. It puts others on notice of your claim to a work. It is also required before an infringement suit can go to court. Additional damages of certain types can be recovered if a work is registered within three months of its creation. Be aware that with the help of an attorney not all claims need to go to court. A letter from an attorney citing the infringement can often put a stop to the problem and possibly lead to settlement negotiations.

Reproduction Rights:

This is the right to reproduce your original work. When you create an original work, you have the sole right to reproduce it until you grant someone else that right through licensing. When licensing a work, it is not necessary to grant the entire copyright. Rather, you may license the right to use it according to a specific contractual agreement (i.e. for a defined purpose and amount of time). Because you retain the right to reproduce your work, you can create prints even if the original art is sold.

Visual Artists Rights Act (VARA):

This act provides "moral rights" to artists who create "works of visual art". These rights give artists doing visual work the right to protect their work separately from and in addition to traditional copyright protection. VARA protection only applies to photographs created for exhibition, paintings, prints, and sculptures. To qualify, the work must be a single copy or in a limited edition of two hundred copies or less, signed, and consecutively numbered by the artist.

7

How Prints Relate to Your Career

Reaching and Identifying Your Target Market

Build a Collection

Pricing Guidelines

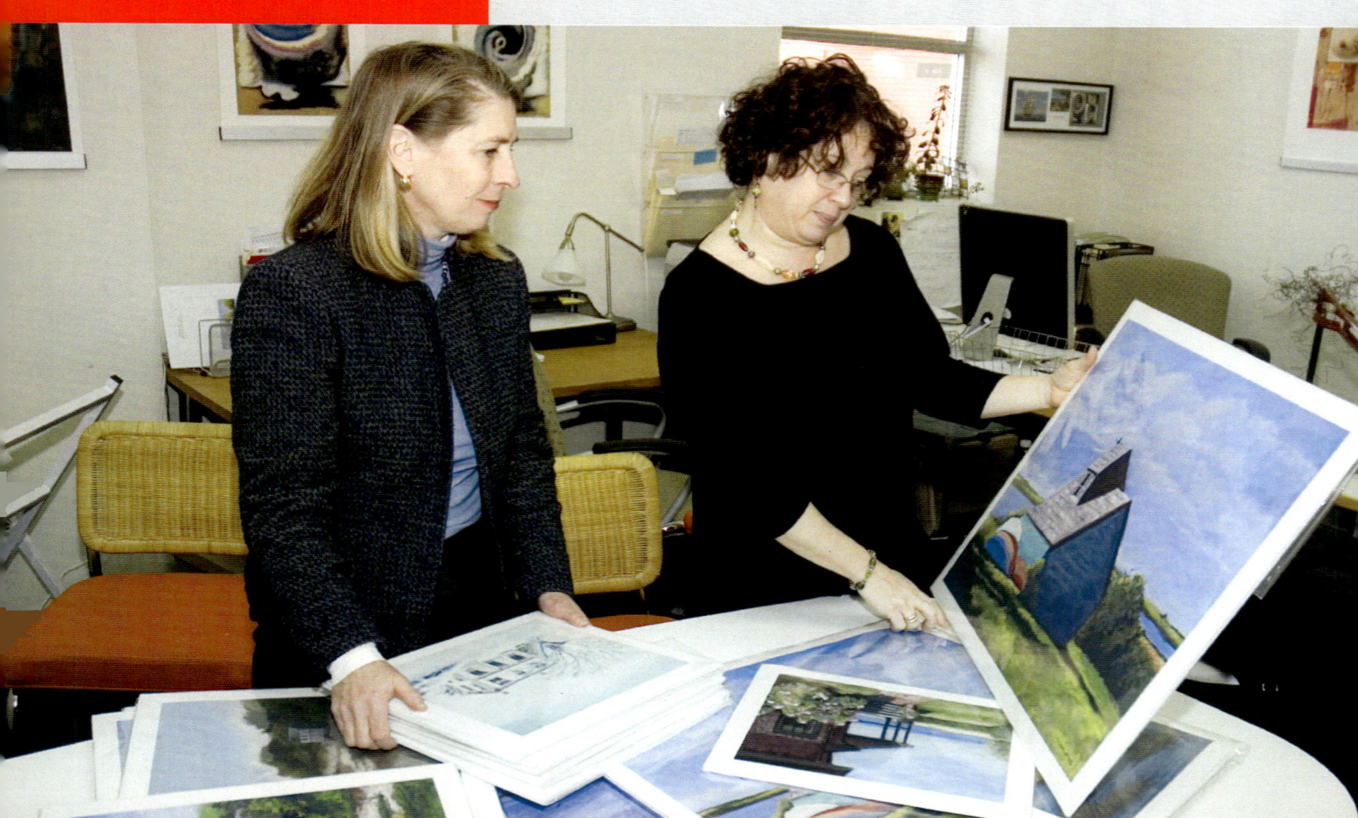

How Marketing Prints Can Advance Your Career

No matter what point you've reached in your evolution as an artist, selling high-quality prints of your originals can help advance your career. For example, let's look at how fine art reproductions can benefit the beginner artist, the part-time artist, and the established full-time artist.

How Prints Relate To Your Career

The Beginner Artist:

If you've just graduated from art school and want to start building a name for yourself, making a few reproductions of your best work can be a great way to get the ball rolling. Going through the entire process, from selecting which pieces to print to selling them, can greatly increase your confidence and help you develop a better understanding of some of the business skills that will be needed to build a sustainable career.

Part-Time Artist:

There are probably many real-life reasons why you cannot devote as much time as you might like to developing your art career. For example, family responsibilities or work may limit the amount of time you have to concentrate on your art. In these circumstances, even the most impassioned artist can find it difficult to create new work or to execute the business and marketing tasks that are needed to keep an art career moving forward. Instead of putting your art work on hold, you can create and sell reproductions of those pieces that gave you the confidence to want to pursue an art career in the first place. If you actively market reproductions of your work, you will keep your name out in front of buyers and continue to make new contacts. Then, when you are able to devote more time to your art, you will not have to start from scratch. Creating digital fine art reproductions of your best work, your art career can continue through constant exposure.

In my experience, the most wonderful outcome for full or part-time artists, is when their recognition grows through the dissemination of their prints. It is something I have witnessed many times. If you are questioning how you will find the time to sell prints, the answer is simple. Showing your prints to family, friends and co-workers is a great way to gain confidence in selling your art. From there you can gradually expand to finding other selling possibilities and revenues.

Taking the critical first step of deciding which works to reproduce will force you to think about your work in a whole new way. It can be a real eye-opener when you start to evaluate which works you personally like best compared to those pieces that might have broader appeal. The whole exercise of selecting work for printing can also help you clarify your personal goals and better identify your target market.

Digital fine art reproduction allows the artist to order on an "as need basis," so a large investment of money is not necessary. As your work matures or as you learn more about which of your images are most popular, you can easily refine your print offerings. Even though a limited edition number may already be set, you always have the option of taking a particular image out of circulation. Without making a huge financial commitment, you can "test market" your work and hone your marketing skills.

An experienced printmaker will consider where you are in your career and help guide you without requiring large print minimums. A reputable printmaker understands that if he can help you achieve reasonable success, then you are more likely to remain a satisfied client for years to come. Your success is also his success!

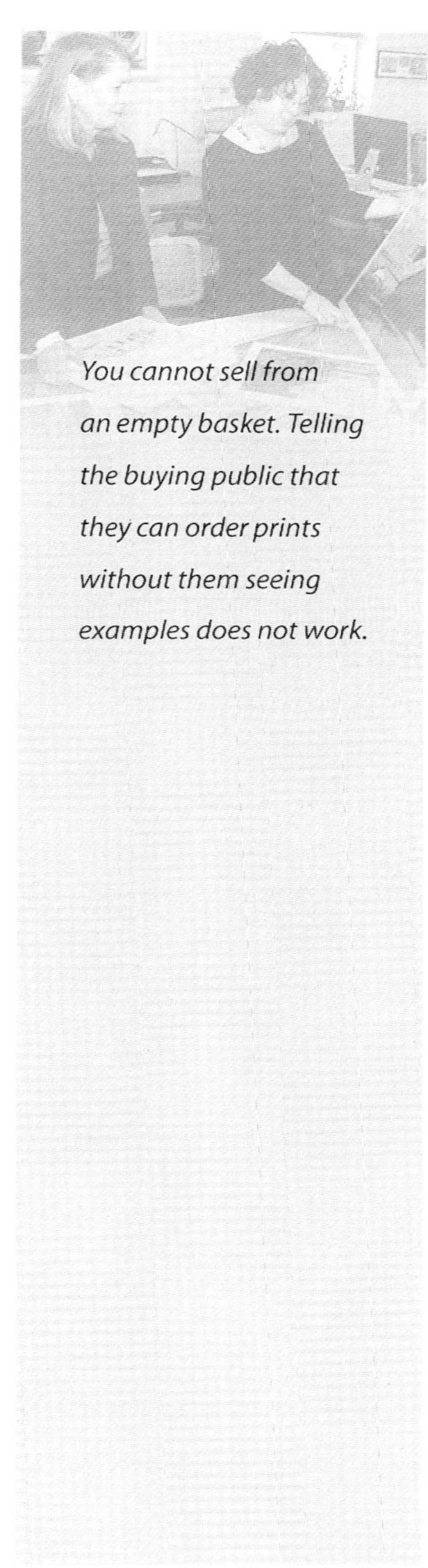

You cannot sell from an empty basket. Telling the buying public that they can order prints without them seeing examples does not work.

If art is your full-time career and you have won some acclaim by regularly showing and selling your work, there are numerous reasons for printing reproductions. For starters, you can increase your exposure by providing high-quality prints to the galleries that will accept them (a trend that is increasing) or selling privately. You may also choose to donate a high-quality reproduction in lieu of the original to fundraising events such as art auctions. You may also want to mass-market reproductions in conjunction with an art publishing company. Art publishers sell your work to retail stores, certain galleries, and framers. Sometimes, an art publisher will use a digital capture and proof provided by the artist that was created by another printmaker, but this is rare. Most art publishers will make their own files and print the work themselves. Expect to see a print quality difference when working with a publisher who is focused on mass marketing vs. a printmaker whose business is geared toward providing individual artists with high quality prints in small editions.

As a full-time artist, you probably have more time for experimentation. For example, some artists are exploring the many ways digital prints can be used to create new originals. This can lead to some inspiring new directions such as printing on unexpected or nontraditional materials, working on your prints with different mediums, or using the print as just one component of an entirely new work of art. For more on this topic, see "Tips for Increasing Value" in Chapter 8.

Reaching and Identifying Your Target Market

Understanding the demographics of who is most likely to be interested in your work is just as important to an artist's success as it is to a filmmaker or the manufacturer of a consumer product. This is not to suggest that you should select the market and then create work to reach that audience. Rather, it is wise to think about who might be the ideal buyer of the work you enjoy creating. If you do not feel comfortable doing it on your own, seek the perspective and advice of a professional in the art business.

One way to start honing in on your ideal buyer is to examine your previous sales. This requires documenting who purchases your art. In addition to keeping track of what each customer purchases and how much they spend, make notes about age, adress, and lifestyle. Also, think about your most successful shows. Who attended? Who purchased? And what attracted them to attend the show? When you analyze this data, a narrative of your market will become apparent. If you have not done this type of survey before, it is a good habit to get into. Go back at least two years and then continue doing so for every sale going forward.

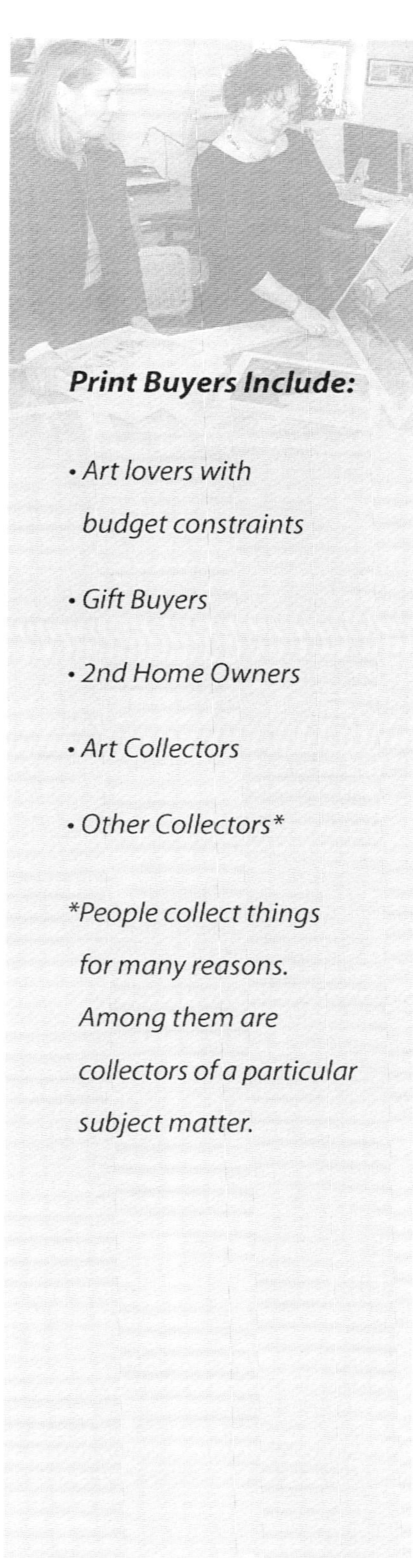

With this knowledge you will be able to increase your sales. Additionaly, you will be more aware of which pieces sell best to your market this will make you better able to choose which prints to reproduce.

To market your prints start out using marketing techniques with which you are already familiar. If you need to grow your marketing skills to broaden your exposure, be sure to allow sufficient time to learn the new skills. You will also need perseverance and patience to achieve your desired long-term results. Keep in mind that you are launching a new division of your art business. In order to be successful, you must be ready to spend some time and have the correct attitude to build awareness, interest, and sales.

Build A Collection

By nature people like choices so it is important to build a collection of images to sell as reproductions. Offering only one image is not recommended, nor is it a reasonable plan for success.

The most commonly asked question is "How do I decide which of my work to print?". First focus on one body of work at a time. For instance, if you work in oil and in watercolor, choose one. If you work only in oils but in a variety of vastly different subjects or styles it is best to begin by considering only one as you complete the worksheet.

Filling out the worksheets that are included may help simplify the process for you. Before beginning think about the following:

- What is my best work? Which pieces receive the most attention?
- Does the group of work contain enough "strong" pieces to offer a good selection?
- What work has the broadest consumer appeal to your target market?

Fill out the following worksheets thinking about the body of work you selected as your focus. To complete this exercise it is best if photographs (or the originals) of each piece are available for reference. Do not work from memory.

Before working with these worksheets you may want to make multiple copies of each for continued use.

ART SUMMARY

Describe why have you selected this collection to offer as signed limited editions. This will help prepare you for talking with potential buyers.

SELECTING THE FEATURED WORKS

List the first 6 pieces you would begin offering as prints. Write why you have chosen each.

1.

2.

3.

4.

5.

6.

DESCRIBE HOW THE SELECTED ART WORKS AS A GROUP

QUALIFYING YOUR CHOICES

Looking at your list of six, and what you have written about them, check off the following.

Does the group look cohesive (like the work of one artist)?

If you have answered "no" or "not sure", explain why.

Yes ☐
No ☐
Not Sure ☐

Does the group present a good variety of quality work?

If you have answered no or not sure explain why.

Yes ☐
No ☐
Not Sure ☐

By doing this exercise you probably find yourself re-thinking your original choices for your print collection. This is a good thing, all it means is that you are beginning to think of your self as an artist in business and a smart marketer, both are necessary for successful selling of prints or originals!

If you have found yourself questioning your choices, or have developed definite views on problems within the group, simply EDIT! Starting all over again is fine too.

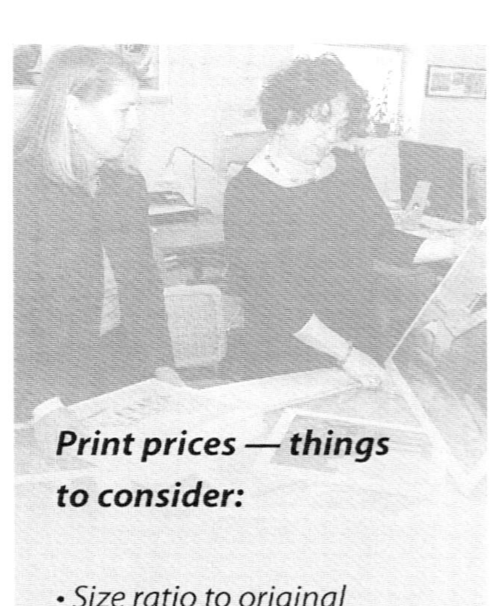

Pricing Guidelines

Even artists with many years of experience struggle with the question of pricing. As with originals, there are no hard-and-fast rules for pricing prints. However, there are steps you can take to guide you in making decisions that are realistic and that will help your career to grow.

First, do your homework by going to art shows and doing some research. Pick shows that feature the work of artists that you emulate or perceive as peers. In addition, visit venues that are most appropriate for your work. Attend openings and examine the work: How does it compare to yours in style, size, quality, and price?

When comparing prices take into consideration the size and media. For example, it would not be accurate to compare the price of your 16 x 20 inch print to a 30 x 40 inch painting. Next, pick up copies of the artist's resume or bio or research the artist on the internet. Your goal is to gain insight into his background and art-related experience. Look for information about age, art education, and the number of years he has worked as a full or part-time artist. Investigate where else the artists has exhibited. Go back before the show ends to see which pieces sold. How does this information correlate with your own history as an artist? For example, keep in mind that one's track record in terms of exposure and sales warrants charging higher print prices.

As you can see, pricing art takes many factors into consideration, and the process is unique to each artist. Use the questions on the following worksheet to help you through the process of self discovery and arrive at pricing that is realistic and well thought out.

Keep in mind that it is fine to start out with prices at one level, and then raise them as your career moves forward. However, it is not good for anyone's career to start too high and then cut prices. Cutting prices sends all the wrong messages. It is like seeing a lot of the same dresses on a sales rack; you sense that there is probably a reason they didn't sell well before the markdowns.

When setting print prices, you are the boss. Established artists have more options for pricing; in some cases, just their signature adds significant value to a print. So, think about where you are in your career now and where you would like to be in the future. You may want to price your prints conservatively because you are mostly interested in exposing your work to the public or because you are satisfied with earning a certain profit. Just be sure your prices are aligned with your goals before you commit. Generally, prints are priced at one quarter to one third of the cost for the original. Another way to approach print pricing is to triple or quadruple your net cost from the printmaker excluding set up costs. (See worksheet 2).

Once you set your price on a print or an original, it must remain constant no matter whether you are selling prints directly to buyers or through galleries or other sources. If you do sell prints through another source, make sure your prices are high enough to include the commission that the seller will expect for making the sale on your behalf.

PRICING YOUR PRINTS

List each piece selected in the previous exercise. Remember this is a work sheet, and not a final inventory list, so, for a complete look at your list of offerings as a whole, give each print potentially being reproduced in another size and or media its own line. Three lines are provided for each image, it is suggested to limit yourself to three reproduction sizes per image. If reproducing at actual size, that should be considered as one.

Title	Print Media	Print Size	Edition Size	Net Cost	Sell Price	Commission
1.						
2.						
3.						
4.						
5.						
6.						

8

Customer Relationships

Romance Cards

Tips For Increasing Value

A Professional Presentation

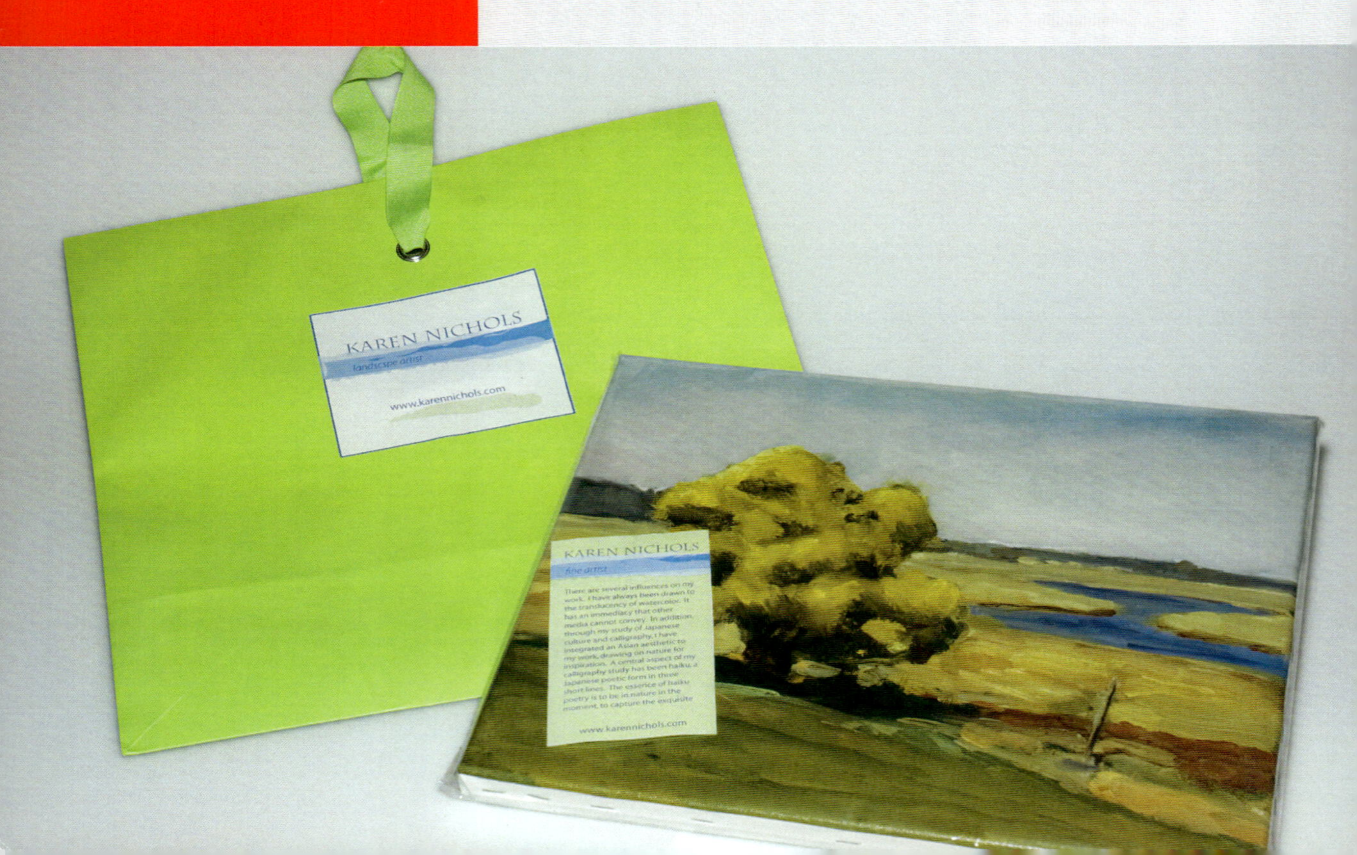

Tips for Successful Selling

The two keys to selling more of your work are: (1) gaining wide exposure for your work through marketing and (2) developing strong relationships with the people who express an interest in your art. This includes keeping your current customers satisfied and adding special touches that make your buyers feel as though they are buying a print that is unique and special. Some buyers also like knowing a little more about the artist who created the work and *some* of the "story" behind each piece. The degree and manner in which you display and package your work can also affect how successful you are in selling your prints.

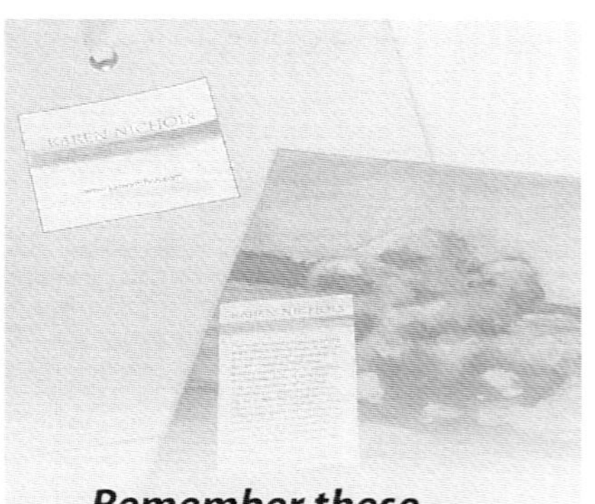

Remember these...

- *New buyers are tomorrows repeat customers.*

- *Professional selling practices build respect.*

- *A great presentation makes you memorable.*

- *Carefully planned marketing gets attention.*

- *When speaking with potential buyers remain friendly but concise.*

Customer Relationships

Developing strong relationships with customers is a quick way to build your reputation. Providing customer service that is "remarkable" will give satisfied customers a reason to talk about you with their friends, relatives, and associates. Other things that will keep customers coming back to you include professional business practices and added value services that go beyond what a buyer might ordinarily expect. In the art world, a fan of your art can often become a valuable friend as well as an avid supporter. Here are some ways to build those relationships:

- While selling a piece of your art, listen carefully to the customers' comments and questions. You'll pick up some clues you can use to overcome any doubts they might be having. For example, if they are not sure how the piece might look on a certain wall, offer to bring the piece to their home or office so they can see for themselves how it would look.

- If a customer is making a large purchase (physical size or monetary value), offer to deliver it.

■ Offer to meet the buyer at the framer's to help select the right frame. This type of gesture will make you memorable to the framer as well.

These "extras" make your buyers feel valued. These additional services can be very worthwhile. Never think of them as an inconvenience or waste of your time. Rather, regard these services as investments in building your career. Over time, it is goodwill that can set you apart from other artists.

Romance Cards

I often advise artists to create what I refer to as a "romance card." This is simply a small card (4 x 6 inches or 5 x 7 inches) that you include with each print you sell. These cards do not have to be elaborate. In fact, you can print them on your desktop printer, but be sure to keep the writing concise and simple and the layout organized and appealing.

Below are some suggestions regarding what to include on the card:

■ **A small photograph of yourself**: Use a photo that shows you working on a piece in your studio. This is better than a head shot because your buyer will like seeing you in your milieu. The in-studio shot will also help position you as the working artist that you are.

■ **A brief bio**: Only use information that relates to you as an artist. You do not need to include where you live, your age, children, or any other non-art related careers or interests.

■ **Some information about your prints**: If you wish to have individual romance cards for each image you make available as a print, then this portion of your card needs to be specific to the piece it accompanies. Romance cards are also a good way to include the edition number, the date, the title, and another signature which adds additional value. For a generic card, make lines that can be filled in for each print.

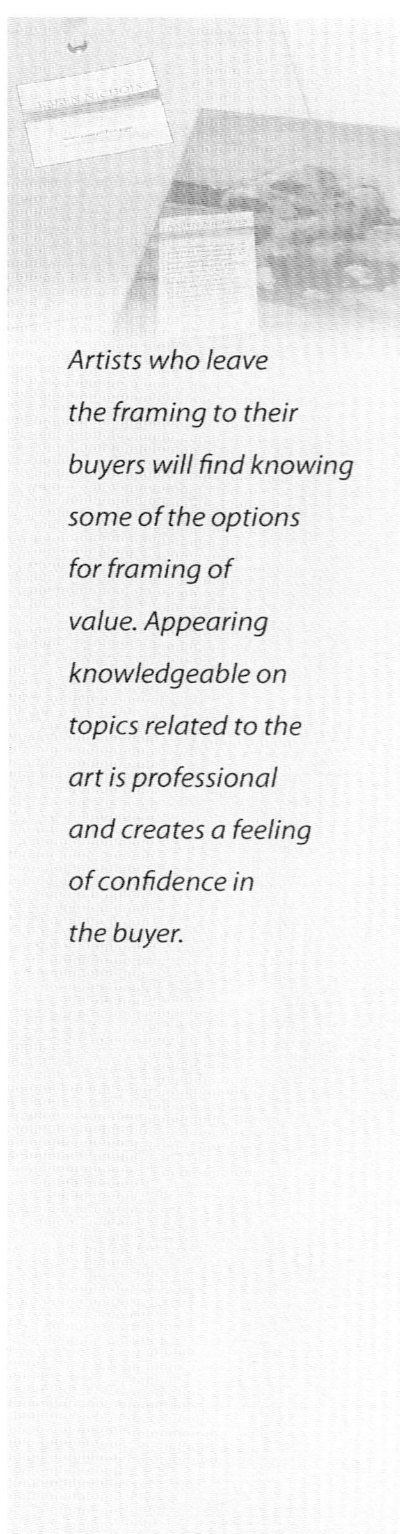

Tips for Increasing Value

Other ways to make each print unique and personal include annotations and remarking. Buyers regard these personal touches as special gestures that can add value to their purchase.

Annotations:

This term simply refers to an additional signature on the back of a canvas or in the margins of a print on paper. An annotation can also include specific information such as a special occasion or fundraiser associated with where or why the print was purchased and by whom.

Remarking:

This concept goes back to the late 19th century when it was common for artists to create a small drawing in the margin of a print. This touch makes each print unique and adds value because the drawing is made by the artist's hand. Printed drawings in the margin do not carry the same cache.

Another method of remarking a print is to add an artist rendered detail to the image that was not in the original. Perhaps this could be a bug in a nature piece or simply a stroke of color that follows a form. I have seen artists use pastels on a watercolor print or gold or silver leafing on canvas or paper prints. Adding an extra detail is not the same as using paints to enhance the printed image or hand-embellishing a print with clear gels or acrylics to add texture to the surface of the print. Neither of these techniques should be necessary in a well-made reproduction. If the client wants the surface quality of an original, he should buy the original.

Taking additional steps to add surface texture is more commonly done with prints that have been mass produced overseas. Fine art reproductions are not of the same ilk.

A Professional Presentation

In the world of selling, presentation is everything. There are two important points to presentation. One is how the pieces are displayed; the other is how they are packaged when handed over to the buyer. Here are some presentation tips to consider when selling prints at art fairs or open studio events.

Displaying:
Along with the unframed paper prints you have displayed for sale in print bins or racks, always have some framed prints on display. A well-made, framed print will attract more interest to all of your prints and may even create an element of surprise when the viewer learns that it is a print and not an original. Some may be motivated to buy the framed prints, because they are ready to hang. Others may still gravitate to the unframed prints either for budgetary reasons or because they would prefer to pick out their own frames. Seeing a framed print helps the buyer to envision how the print might look in his home or office.

Use the appropriate size bin for your prints. Prints that are too small for the bin can slip out of the rack and tumble to the floor. It also makes flipping through the rack awkward and can make the viewer uncomfortable or even reluctant to look. Bins are available in different sizes including tabletop varieties.

Avoid the common mistake of overfilling the print bin. If you have multiple prints of the same image of the same size, place only one of the prints in the bin at a time. When that one sells, replace it with another.

Whenever possible, hang framed prints. In addition, use easels for display. Good quality, collapsible easels that come in their own cases are the most convenient and tend to be sturdier than light weight, wooden easels. When arranging easels, consider the spacing and viewing angles. Move them around a bit and step back to see how they look to the people who are passing or entering your display area. Try setting the easel at different heights as well. Table easels can be very handy for small works and come in a variety of styles and finishes. For a polished look, stick to one style that best complements your work.

Packaging:

We have already discussed inserting a romance card when you sell a print. Try to visualize how you would like the buyer walking away with your art work to look. The importance of attractive packaging may not always be obvious, but imagine how you would feel if you purchased a special piece of clothing and the seller threw it in a used grocery bag, or worse, just handed the garment over to you. What would you think of that merchant?

The lack of professional packaging implies that the seller does not value the piece you just purchased or you as a customer. Having a pre planned method of wrapping your print is more professional and reflects how highly you regard your own work.

Following are some basic things to consider when developing packaging for your prints:

- **Time and expense**: The materials you choose should be easy to obtain, store, and transport. Have a budget in mind as you develop your idea and research the items you will need. Some materials that work well include cello bags, ribbon, white or color shopping bags, labels for sealing cello bags, or to place on bags.

- **Simplicity**: Keep it simple! Not only will you have to put it all together on the spot, such as at an art fair, but your customer will also have to walk around with it and transport the work home without damaging it.

■ **Exposure**: Stores go to the added expense of printing their names on their shopping bags for added exposure. As your customer walks through a show with your name on a purchase that is tastefully, creatively, and conveniently packaged, it will draw further attention to your success as an artist. Not only will it help promote you as a professional, but it will show that you are an artist whose work is selling, so, incorporate labeling into your packaging.

Afterward

Now that you have read this book, I hope you will remember that it was intended primarily to give artists an overview of digital fine art reproduction as it exists at the time of this book's publication.

As the popularity of digitally reproducing art increases, it is important for artists to be aware that the process is still evolving.

Artists today can make a difference; think of yourselves as contributing to the next step in fine art reproduction. Like artists who helped prior technologies develop, you can also by setting high expectations with your printmaker and, therefore, standards of quality, and by helping educate art buyers.

New technology will continue to be introduced, and some will successfully provide an even wider range of options. However, it is the creator of the original art, (the artist) who should ultimately determine what is an acceptable reproduction. Set your standards high. You should be no different today than Rubens or Titian in the 17th century who sought out the very best engravers to work exclusively with them as a way to control their reproduction quality.

Ordering Instructions

To order more books, please visit www.artistsgicleehandbook.com

Glossary: A-Z

A

acid free (paper)
Refers to paper that does not contain acids. Acids can cause paper to discolor, become inflexible, and eventually turn brittle over time. Acid free paper is commonly used for fine art prints and limited edition printing because paper acidity will harm the image.

annotation
A commentary, explanation, or interpretation about the drawing or work you have produced. It adds value and uniqueness to your artwork.

archival
A term that has been used extensively in conservation literature but that lacks an internationally accepted definition. Generally it refers to characteristics of long term stability (as in: archival quality). Considered meaningless unless qualified with additional information, data, etc.

archiving
Retention of final images, often on CD-ROM for reprinting. Information necessary to reproduce the print is also archived including sizes and media used.

artist's proof
One of a small group of prints set aside from the edition for the artist's use. Printer's proofs are sometimes also done for the printer's records.

aqueous inks
Aqueous inks used in ink jet printing processes are comprised mainly of water and contain a hydrophilic organic solvent, coloring, and various nonsolvent additives. However, more recently developed aqueous ink may include solvents as well.

B

balanced lighting
Optically balanced light is the closest you can get to the optics of natural light. Best used for high resolution scanning and proofing.

bon-a-tirer or BAT (bone-ah-ti-ray)
An artist approved proof that is used as the standard for comparing all subsequent prints. Some printers require a signed BAT before production printing can begin.

C

capture
Acquiring information such as an image with a digital scanning device.

closed loop
Closed loop calibration is a method of color calibrating all hardware and software used in the print process to ensure that scanned and printed colors match the colors on the original accurately.

coating
The process of treating media or substrates to accept inkjet inks. Also, a thin "coating" applied to prints on canvas to add durability and contains some UV protection as well.

cold press paper
Watercolor paper made in a mold, roughly textured, also available with an ink-jet coating for digital printmaking.

color balance
Refers to the overall colors in relation to each other. The ability to reproduce the colors of an original accurately and without color cast.

color calibration
Software and/or hardware used by the printmaker to adjust and coordinate colors between two or more digital devices.

color cast
The predominance of a particular color which affects the whole image due to an excess of a color pigment or of light.

color management (color profiles)
A combination of advanced software and/or hardware devices used to produce accurate color results throughout a digital imaging system.

color space
The parts of the visible spectrum which can be reproduced in a given medium (i.e., RGB for computer monitors, CMYK for print, web safe index colors for the web).

color temperature
A manufacturer's method of indicating the color of a light source in degrees Kelvin (K); 5500K (blue/white), is ideal for the digital and reproduction process.

continuous tone
A photographic image containing gradient tones without screens.

copyright
Legal basis for the owner's control of the usage of his or her images or artworks.

crop
To remove part of an image.

D

digital art
Using a digital processes or technologies to create art.

digital commercial printing
A printer who uses digital technology to print promotional, advertising, and other such materials.

digital fine art print
A fine art print made by a digital process excluding older technologies such as film.

digital fine art reproduction printmaker
A person producing reproduction prints from the artist approved master file and under the artist's supervision. Originally, engravers and lithographers created the master plate from which reproductions were made.

digital imaging
The process of image capture and manipulation accomplished by digital systems.

digital media
The common term used for all digital printing substrates. Does not indicate type or stability.

digital "noise"
The digital equivalent of film grain found in film photography. In digital images, this noise appears as random speckles and can significantly degrade image quality. Noise increases when incorrect lighting leads to long exposures or with high ISO settings.

digital printer
A device that is capable of translating digital data into hard copy output. Typically refers to ink-jet or laser printing.

digital (SLR) camera
A digital camera that uses a mechanical mirror system and pentaprism to direct light from the lens to an optical viewfinder on the back of the camera. Rather than using film, a digital camera records the image to a chip.

digitize
The process of converting analog data to digital information.

DPI (density per inch)

DPI is printer resolution; it is
not image resolution, although
frequently used that way. Rather,
it is a measure of the resolution of a
printer. It properly refers to the dots
of ink (or toner) used by an ink-jet
printer (or other printing device).
In general, the more dots, the better
and sharper the image. For print,
image files are optimized at 300 DPI.
For the Web, GIF, and JPEG file
formats, files are optimized at 72
to 300 DPI.

D Roller

Used to take the curl out of a piece
of paper. Consists of a heavy metal
tube with a large sheet of plastic
wrapped around it. The print is
rolled up starting from the heavy
metal end causing the print to roll
counter to its curl.

drum scanner

A type of optical scanner where the
art is mounted to a rotating drum. As
the drum spins, the image rotates
past a fixed lens or sensor allowing
the image to be recorded as a series
of fine lines.

drum scanning

Originally designed for scanning
transparencies and negatives.

E

edition

The sum of identical prints of the
same size on the same substrate
produced from a single image
printed at one time or on demand.,
(see also "open edition" and
"limited edition").

engraving

A method of engraving in a steel
plate, developed by Thomas Lupton
in 1822, which allows for finer detail
and many more impressions than
copper.

etching

An etching (also called a line
etching) is created by covering a
metal plate with an acid-resistant
layer of wax called a ground and then
drawing a design through the
ground using an etching needle. The
plate is then dipped in acid which
bites into the exposed lines, thus,
etching the design into the plate.

F

film

Photographic material consisting
of a base of celluloid covered
with emulsion.

fine art

The products of human creativity;
works of art collectively.

fine art print
A print conceived and executed by an artist by means of a fine art print process.

flatbed scanner
A type of optical scanner that consists of a flat surface on which you lay documents to be scanned.

G

gallery wrap
A method of stretching an artist's canvas so that the canvas wraps around the sides and is secured to the back of the wooden frame.

gamut
The range of colors provided by a specific input or output device or by a set of inks.

H

highlight
Light areas within an image. Also called "specular reflection" or "hot spots".

hot press
Process for making smooth textured art paper in a mold, also available with an inkjet coating for digital print making.

I

iteration
A single execution of a set of instructions that are to be repeated.

inkjet/ inkjet printer
A digital printing technology that uses nozzles to spray ink onto a surface.

IRIS or IRIS print
The branded inkjet printer that produced the early "digital fine art prints" and for which the term "giclée" was first used. Currently no longer being manufactured.

J

jpeg (joint photographic experts group)
Standardized image compression format developed by the Joint Photographic Experts Group.

L

large-format printer
In digital fine art, a printer that prints on large paper which can range from 24" to 64" inch width. Such printers typically use inkjet technology to print on a variety of digital media.

large format camera
Preferred by professional digital
fine art reproduction printmakers
because of its ability to create
the extremely high resolution
files necessary for quality art
reproduction.

limited edition prints
A number of multiples all depicting
the same image in which a limit is
placed on the number of impressions
(prints) created. Limited editions are
usually numbered and are most
often signed.

lithography
The process of printing from a stone
or metal plate on which the image to
be printed is ink-receptive and the
blank area is ink repellent. The process
is based on the principle that grease
and water do not mix. Commercial
lithograph printing uses plates and is
capable of producing large runs.

M

margin
The blank space bordering the
printed area of a print.

media
The common term used in digital
printing for substrate; the surface
to be printed on such as fine art
papers, canvas, and other ink-jet
coated materials.

medium format camera
Commercial photographers prefer a
medium format camera because it
exposes a larger image area.

monoprint
One of a series in which each print
has some differences of color, design,
texture, etc. making each print
unique.

museum glass
An antieflection picture framing glass
for art. Along with its nearly invisible
finish, it effectively blocks up to 99%
of harmful indoor and outdoor UV
light rays so framed pieces remain
clearer and brighter for longer.

N

nonglare glass
A picture framing glass is finished
to diffuse reflected light. This
process also gives the glass surface
a matte finish. Non-glare glass cuts
down on the amount of light
reaching the print.

O

optical brighteners (OBs)
Also referred to as a "fluorescent
brightener" a chemical agent added
to paper during the manufacturing
stage for the purpose of making the
paper appear whiter (or "brighter").

offset printing (offset lithography)
The most common commercial printing method. Ink is "offset" from the printing plate to a rubber roller then to paper. Capable of long continuous runs.

open edition
An edition or set of identical prints from a single master that is not limited in number (see also "edition" and "limited edition").

out gassing
The release of adsorbed or occluded gases or water vapor.

P

pixel
Derived from pi(x)cture element. Refers to the smallest element of the digital image. The more pixels per inch, the higher the resolution.

plexiglass
A transparent plastic used as a substitute for glass. Frames with plexiglass offer better impact resistance than glass.

PPI (pixels per inch)
A measure of resolution or density of pixels in a digital image.

print
In the context of art, an original work of art (woodcut, etching, serigraph, photograph, etc.) where artwork does not exist until it is printed. The print is made directly from a master surface made by the artist. Also known as "fine art print," "work on paper," and "original print". A print is one in a set of all the impressions made from the same master image.

print on demand
The ability of digital printing to produce identical prints individually or sporadically over any period of time allowing small numbers of prints to be ordered as needed.

printing
The process of applying ink to a substrate.

profile
In digital printing a file of data generally used to refer, to a color profile of a specific piece of equipment (monitor, printer, scanner, etc.) that enables the user to correlate color consistently on various devices.

proof

A proof is an impression of a print pulled prior to the regular, published edition. In fine art printing. as well as in digital fine art reproduction, proofs are pulled so that the artist (and printmaker) can see what work still needs to be done to the master. The final proof is often signed by the artist to indicate approval and is used for comparison purposes by the printer. An artist's proof is an impression issued in addition to the regularly numbered edition and reserved for the artist's own use. (see "bon à tirer").

proofing

The process used to obtain hard-copy output directly from a master surface or digital files for purposes of predicting the appearance of a final print. The process is repeated until the artist is satisfied.

proofing paper

Traditionally used in commercial printing, proofing paper simulates the glossy commercial printing process by providing a high resolution image with high color saturation and instant drying for easy handling. However, it is not appropriate for use in digital fine art reproduction where only the actual media planned for the edition should be used.

provenance

A record of origin and/or ownership of a work of art used as a guide to authenticity or quality.

R

rag papers

In fine art printmaking and digital reproduction, rag (cotton) refers to paper, high quality paper.

reflective art

Artwork that is neither digital nor transparent. Refers to artwork with the light on the same side of the image as the viewer.

remarque

A remarque is a small vignette image in the margin of a print often related thematically to the main image. Originally, remarques were scribbled sketches made in the margins of etchings. During the late nineteenth century, remarques became popular as an additional design element in prints.

reproduction

A copy of an original work of art. In the context of digital art, a copy of artwork that already exists in some other original art form. Prints resulting from digital photography or art created using a computer (digital art) are not considered reproductions.

resolution
Refers to the number of pixels. A measurement of the "fineness" of digital detail, pixels per inch or pixel density (see "DPI" and "PPI").

RGB
A color model using red, green, and blue; the additive primary colors. Video display systems use RGB data to create screen images. Used on monitors for viewing and color correcting images before conversion to CMYK for the final digital print.

RIP (Raster Image Processor)
Software allowing the computer to give specific instructions to the printer. In quality digital reproduction, it includes the use of custom profiles for color-calibration specific to the media and the printer it will run on (see profiles) .

S

scan
The process of translating a picture from reflective art into digital information.

scanner
Hardware that illuminates, reads, and then converts original text, artwork, or film into digital data. Types of scanners include flatbed, film, and drum.

scanning back
A high quality digital device back for medium or large format cameras which scans creating a digital recording pixel by pixel of the subject. Large format cameras with a 300 mega pixel scanning back specific to digital fine art reproduction is the tool of choice for the best results.

screen printing
Ink is applied directly to the surface to be printed. The image to be printed is photographically transferred to a very fine fabric (the screen). Non printing areas are blocked off and the ink is then wiped across the screen to pass through the unblocked pores to reach the substrate. For each color to be printed a separate screen is prepared and the process is repeated.

sharpening
A digital enhancement making more distinct borders, areas, lines, or tones. Considered standard procedure; however, "over-sharpening" can affect the final print appearance.

signed

A signed print is one signed in pencil or in another appropriate medium by the artist. In the late nineteenth century, in response to the development of photomechanical reproduction techniques, fine arts prints were signed by the artists in order to distinguish between original prints and reproductions. Today, the artist's signature on a reproduction is for authenticity and added value.

SLR

Single Lens Reflex, a form of small format (35 mm) camera that has a reflecting mirror that retracts when the shutter is released. An SLR digital camera allows the photographer to view the image exactly as it will be framed in the photo.

solvent ink

This term is used to describe any ink that is not water-based.

spectral highlight (digital)

An area or a spot in a photograph or scan that is strongly illuminated usually resulting from reflection of a light source. Digital imaging of artwork can eliminate the highlights using specific professional means.

stitching (digitally)

The process of perfectly aligning images and combining them to form a larger image.

strobe

An electronically regulated discharge tube that can emit extremely rapid, brief, and brilliant flashes of light: used in photography, the theater, etc. Not recommended for digital imaging of art where a constant light source is required.

substrate

The material that receives the printed image. In digital printing the substrate carries an ink-jet coating and is often referred to as "digital media" (see coating).

T

test market

Test marketing is an important tool for ensuring that the market can accepts your product in terms of quaty and price.

TIFF (Tagged Image Format File)

A file format for saving and storing digital images.